About Math Connection:

Welcome to Rainbow Bridge Publishing's Connection series. Math Connection provides students with focused practice to help reinforce and develop math skills in all areas defined by the NCTM (National Council of Teachers of Mathematics) as appropriate for second-grade students. These include numeration and operations, two- and three-digit addition and subtraction, probability, measurement, shapes, graphing, fractions, time, money values, word problems, and an introduction to multiplication. Exercises are grade-level appropriate with clear examples and instructions to guide the lesson; they also feature a variety of activities to help students develop their ability to work with numbers.

Math Connection • Grade 2
Written by Nancy Bosse

© 2002, 2004 Rainbow Bridge Publishing. All rights reserved.

Permission to Reproduce

Series Creator
Michele Van Leeuwen

Illustrations
Amanda Sorensen

Visual Design and Layout
Andy Carlson, Robyn Funk

Editorial Director
Paul Rawlins

Copy Editors and Proofreaders
Kim Carlson, Melody Feist, Aimee Hansen

Special Thanks
Dante J. Orazzi

Please visit our website at
www.summerbridgeactivities.com
for supplements, additions, and corrections to this book.

Second Edition 2004

ISBN: 1-887923-78-0

PRINTED IN THE UNITED STATES OF AMERICA
10 9 8 7 6 5 4

Math Connection — Grade 2
Table of Contents

...continued

Diagnostic Test 1

Solve the problems.

1.

3	4	6	9	8	2
+ 5	+ 5	+ 1	+ 1	+ 2	+ 3

2.

5	7	6	9	6	8
− 4	− 2	− 3	− 3	− 4	− 5

3.

6	7	8	9	10	6
+ 6	+ 7	+ 8	+ 9	+ 10	+ 7

4.

12	16	15	17	15	18
− 7	− 8	− 9	− 9	− 8	− 9

5.   24 is the same as _____ tens _____ ones

6.   72 is the same as _____ tens _____ ones

Circle the number that is <u>more</u>.

7.   34   35

8.   67   76

Circle the even numbers.

9.   1   2   3   4   5   6   7   8   9   10

10.   22   35   44   56   67   68   70   75   79   86

Math Connection—Grade 2—RBP3780   www.summerbridgeactivities.com   ©RBP Books

Diagnostic Test 2
Solve the problems.

Count the coins. Write the total.

1.

2.

3.

4.

Solve the problems.

5.
10	9	7	12	15	8
+ 7	+ 8	+ 11	+ 6	+ 2	+ 7

6.
18	17	16	14	15	18
− 7	− 10	− 9	− 8	− 6	− 9

7.
2	4	3	5	3	2
3	2	8	6	1	7
+ 7	+ 8	+ 4	+ 2	+ 9	+ 8

Write the times shown on the clocks.

8.

_____ : _____

9.

_____ : _____

10.

_____ : _____

Diagnostic Test 3

Solve the problems.

1. 24 + 12	34 + 23	11 + 46	21 + 67	53 + 16	45 + 21
2. 75 − 11	87 − 24	67 − 33	57 − 32	34 − 12	56 − 30
3. 43 + 28	56 + 27	62 + 19	27 + 37	49 + 24	28 + 18
4. 57 − 18	83 − 26	48 − 29	77 − 39	81 − 26	70 − 19

Count the money. Write the total.

5.

6.

www.summerbridgeactivities.com ©RBP Books

Diagnostic Test 4

Write how many hundreds, tens, and ones.

1. 239 equals _____ hundreds _____ tens _____ ones

2. 803 equals _____ hundreds _____ tens _____ ones

Write the number that comes between.

3. 478 _____ 480

4. 899 _____ 901

Use > or < to make each problem correct.

5. 123 _____ 124   7. 832 _____ 842

6. 794 _____ 749   8. 300 _____ 299

Solve the problems.

9.
$$
\begin{array}{r} 821 \\ + 123 \\ \hline \end{array}
\qquad
\begin{array}{r} 672 \\ + 306 \\ \hline \end{array}
\qquad
\begin{array}{r} 235 \\ + 142 \\ \hline \end{array}
\qquad
\begin{array}{r} 411 \\ + 376 \\ \hline \end{array}
\qquad
\begin{array}{r} 320 \\ + 174 \\ \hline \end{array}
$$

10.
$$
\begin{array}{r} 840 \\ - 320 \\ \hline \end{array}
\qquad
\begin{array}{r} 376 \\ - 134 \\ \hline \end{array}
\qquad
\begin{array}{r} 987 \\ - 235 \\ \hline \end{array}
\qquad
\begin{array}{r} 863 \\ - 351 \\ \hline \end{array}
\qquad
\begin{array}{r} 732 \\ - 600 \\ \hline \end{array}
$$

Diagnostic Test 5
Solve the problems.

1.

238	732	620	376	732
+ 128	+ 170	+ 199	+ 237	+ 248

2.

932	843	377	482	530
− 318	− 129	− 258	− 175	− 107

3.

4	3	5	4	1	2
x 2	x 2	x 3	x 5	x 3	x 4

Measure these lines with a ruler.

4.

= _____ inches

5.

= _____ inches

Circle the fraction that tells how much is shaded.

6.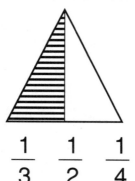

$\frac{1}{3}$ $\frac{1}{2}$ $\frac{1}{4}$

7.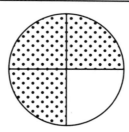

$\frac{1}{4}$ $\frac{2}{4}$ $\frac{3}{4}$

8.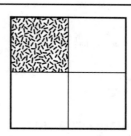

$\frac{1}{4}$ $\frac{1}{2}$ $\frac{1}{3}$

What comes next?

9.

10.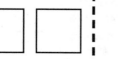

Diagnostic Test Analysis

After you review your student's diagnostic test, match those problems answered incorrectly to the sections below. Pay special attention to the pages that fall into these problem sections and ensure that your student receives supervision in these areas. In this way, your student will strengthen these specific math skills.

Addition and Subtraction Facts

Diagnostic Test 1
Problems 1–4

Diagnostic Test 2
Problems 5–7

Review Pages:
24–43, 60–61

Numeration 0–99

Diagnostic Test 1
Problems 5–10

Review Pages:
10–15

Adding and Subtracting of 2-Digit Numbers

Diagnostic Test 3
Problems 1–4

Review Pages:
62–87

Numeration 100–999

Diagnostic Test 4
Problems 1–8

Review Pages:
16–23

Adding and Subtracting of 3-Digit Numbers

Diagnostic Test 4
Problems 9–10

Review Pages:
97–108

Beginning Multiplication

Diagnostic Test 5
Problem 3

Review Pages:
117–122

Counting Money

Diagnostic Test 2
Problems 1–4

Diagnostic Test 3
Problems 5–6

Review Pages:
44–51, 58–59

Telling Time

Diagnostic Test 2
Problems 8–10

Review Pages:
52–59

Measurement

Diagnostic Test 5
Problems 4–5

Review Pages:
93–96

Fractions

Diagnostic Test 5
Problems 6–8

Review Pages:
109–112

Patterns

Diagnostic Test 5
Problems 9–10

Review Pages:
115–116

Numeration: Tens and Ones

Write how many tens and ones. Then write the number.

  5 tens and 2 ones is the same as 52.

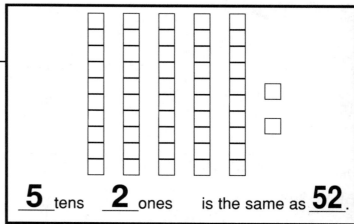

____5___ tens ___2___ ones   is the same as ___52___.

1.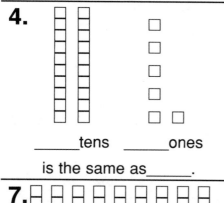

_____tens _____ones

is the same as_____.

2.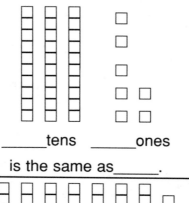

_____tens _____ones

is the same as_____.

3.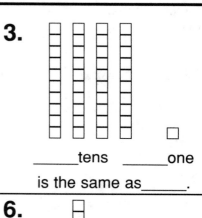

_____tens _____one

is the same as_____.

4.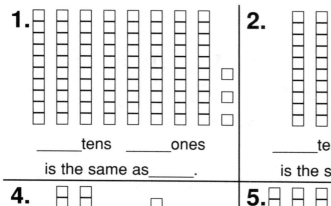

_____tens _____ones

is the same as_____.

5.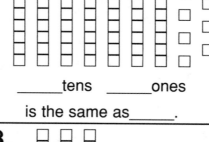

_____tens _____ones

is the same as_____.

6.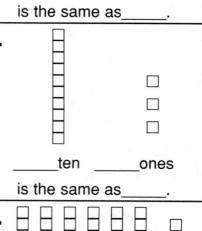

_____ten _____ones

is the same as_____.

7.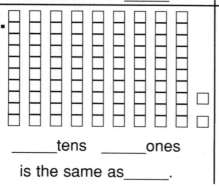

_____tens _____ones

is the same as_____.

8.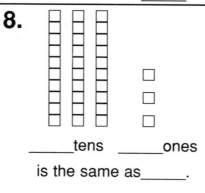

_____tens _____ones

is the same as_____.

9.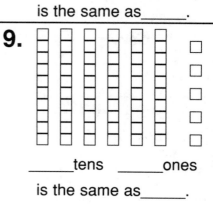

_____tens _____ones

is the same as_____.

Math Connection—Grade 2—RBP3780   www.summerbridgeactivities.com   ©RBP Books

Numeration: Tens and Ones

Write the numbers.

Count the tens first.
Then count the ones.

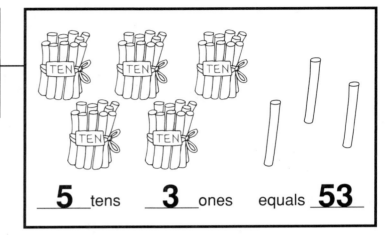

__5__ tens __3__ ones equals __53__

1.

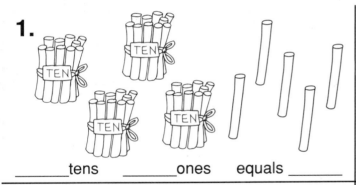

_____tens _____ones equals _____

2.

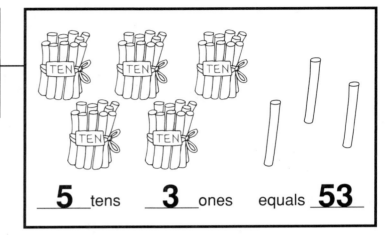

_____tens _____ones equals _____

3.

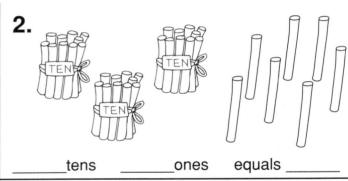

_____tens _____ones equals _____

4.

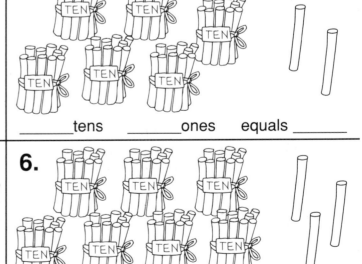

_____tens _____ones equals _____

5.

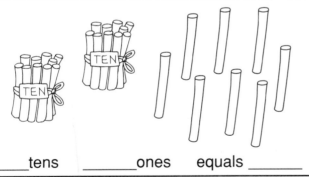

_____tens _____ones equals _____

6.

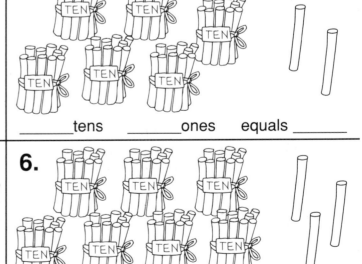

_____tens _____ones equals _____

www.summerbridgeactivities.com **Math Connection—Grade 2—RBP3780**

Numeration: Writing Numbers 0–99

Start with 0. Write to 99.

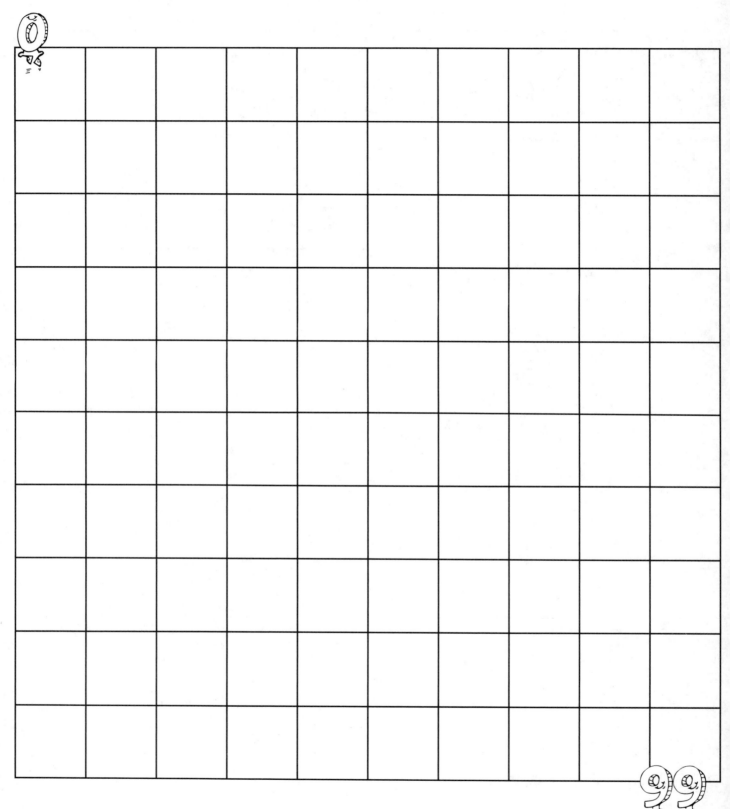

Reading Number Words
Write the number.

Ok, smile and say "Numerals!"

1.

one _____ **1** _____

ten _____

six _____

four _____

nine _____

twelve _____

2.

five _____

zero _____

eleven _____

seven _____

two _____

eight _____

3.

three _____

fourteen _____

thirty _____

sixteen _____

fifty _____

twenty _____

4.

thirty-one _____

thirteen _____

forty-three _____

eighty-nine _____

twenty-four _____

ninety-two _____

5.

seventy-five _____

twenty-nine _____

sixty-seven _____

eighteen _____

sixty-eight _____

fifty-two _____

6.

ninety-nine _____

fifteen _____

eighty-eight _____

one hundred _____

seventeen _____

fifty-four _____

© RBP Books   www.summerbridgeactivities.com   Math Connection—Grade 2—RBP3780

Comparing Numbers 1–99

Look at the tens first,
then the ones.

I bet you can do
this exercise
in a snap!

Circle the number that is <u>more</u>.

1.		2.		3.	
14	(19)	10	9	79	42
16	17	11	6	67	94
12	8	30	31	25	26
17	18	15	7	87	78

Circle the number that is <u>less</u>.

4.		5.		6.	
30	20	21	31	88	86
52	25	85	84	76	67
40	41	39	40	39	93

Math Connection—Grade 2—RBP3780   www.summerbridgeactivities.com   ©RBP Books

Odd, Even, and Ordinal Numbers

 Even numbers are 2, 4, 6, 8, and so on.
Odd numbers are 1, 3, 5, 7, and so on.
Ordinal numbers are *first*, *second*, and so on.

Color the bubbles.

Color the bubbles with odd numbers red. Color the bubbles with even numbers yellow.

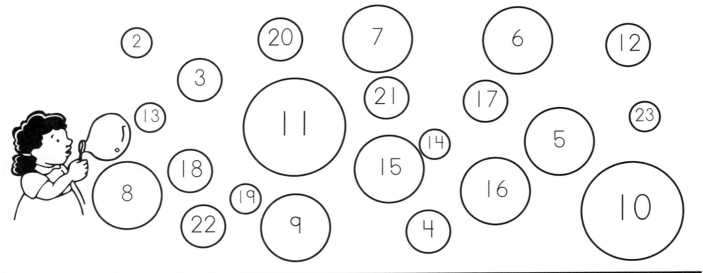

 Grayson   Allie   Denise   Tanner   Lori   Matt   Rob

1. Who is third in line? _____.

2. Who is sixth in line? _____.

3. Who is seventh? _____.

4. Who is second? _____.

5. Who is fourth? _____.

Numeration: Hundreds, Tens, and Ones

Write how many hundreds, tens, and ones. Then write the total.

1.

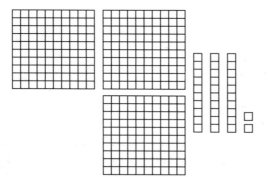

____3___ hundreds ___3___ tens ___2___ ones
is the same as___**332**___.

2.

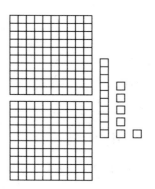

_____ hundreds _____ ten _____ ones
is the same as_____.

3.

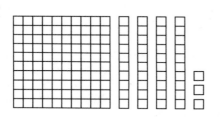

_____ hundred _____ tens _____ ones
is the same as_____.

4.

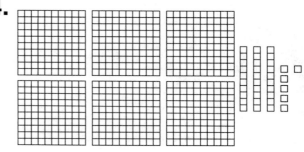

_____ hundreds _____ tens _____ one
is the same as_____.

5.

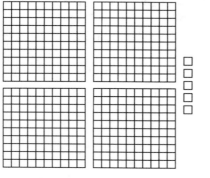

_____ hundreds _____ tens _____ ones
is the same as_____.

6.

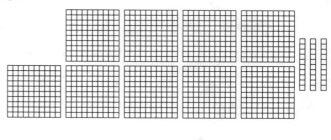

_____ hundreds _____ tens _____ ones
is the same as_____.

Math Connection—Grade 2—RBP3780   www.summerbridgeactivities.com   ©RBP Books

Numeration: Hundreds, Tens, and Ones

OK, now who ordered the 221?

Write how many hundreds, tens, and ones.

1.   129   _____hundred   _____tens   _____ones

2.   936   _____hundreds   _____tens   _____ones

3.   462   _____hundreds   _____tens   _____ones

4.   248   _____hundreds   _____tens   _____ones

5.   320   _____hundreds   _____tens   _____ones

6.   863   _____hundreds   _____tens   _____ones

Write the number.

7.   2 hundreds, 6 tens, 4 ones   =   _____

8.   7 hundreds, 8 tens, 2 ones   =   _____

9.   9 hundreds, 1 ten, 4 ones   =   _____

10.   1 hundred, 5 tens, 3 ones   =   _____

11.   3 hundreds, 0 tens, 5 ones   =   _____

12.   3 hundreds, 7 tens, 6 ones   =   _____

   www.summerbridgeactivities.com   Math Connection—Grade 2—RBP3780

Numeration: Hundreds, Tens, and Ones

Follow the directions below.

1. 8 3 4   Circle the number in the ones place.
            Put a square around the number in the tens place.

2. 5 2 7   Circle the number in the tens place. Put a triangle
            around the number in the hundreds place.

3. 9 0 9   Put a circle around the number in the ones place.
            Put a square around the number in the
            hundreds place.

4. 2 4 1   Put a square around the number in the tens place.
            Circle the number in the hundreds place, and draw a
            triangle around the number in the ones place.

5. 1 5 6   Make a circle around the number in the tens place.
            Make a triangle around the number in the ones
            place.

6. 3 1 7   Draw a square around the number in the hundreds
            place. Cross out the number in the tens place.
            Circle the number in the ones place.

7. 6 6 2   Put a triangle around the number in the ones place.
            Cross out the number in the tens place, and put a
            square around the number in the hundreds place.

8. 4 8 5   Circle the number in the hundreds place.
            Put a square around the number in the ones place.

Math Connection—Grade 2—RBP3780   www.summerbridgeactivities.com   ©RBP Books

Numbers 100–999

 Think about the number that comes before, between, and after each number. Count in your head if you need to.

	Before		Between		After	
1.	**346**	347	213	___ 215	679	___
2.	___	528	427	___ 429	721	___
3.	___	832	399	___ 401	398	___
4.	___	731	478	___ 480	599	___
5.	___	293	871	___ 873	734	___
6.	___	799	587	___ 589	500	___
7.	___	123	700	___ 702	399	___
8.	___	423	129	___ 131	790	___
9.	___	987	699	___ 701	439	___
10.	___	844	989	___ 991	287	___

Comparing Numbers 100–999

 Look at the hundreds column first, then the tens, then the ones. Nine tens is more than 0 tens, so 890 is more than 809.

809   **890**

Circle the number that is <u>more</u>.

1. 334   434
2. 567   765
3. 823   832
4. 790   709

5. 120   210
6. 478   874
7. 612   621
8. 909   908

Circle the number that is <u>less</u>.

9. 119   191
10. 345   435
11. 812   810
12. 923   933

13. 608   680
14. 599   600
15. 218   219
16. 710   719

Comparing Numbers 100–999

Use >, <, or = to make each problem correct.

=	>	<
means equal to	means more than	means less than

The arrow points to the smaller number and opens wide to the larger number. 352 > 325 means 352 is more than 325.

1. 435   [<]   453

2. 712   [   ]   721

3. 821   [   ]   811

4. 741   [   ]   471

5. 125   [   ]   215

6. 345   [   ]   345

7. 794   [   ]   798

8. 412   [   ]   421

9. 223   [   ]   232

10. 528   [   ]   528

Numeration Assessment

Write how many hundreds, tens, and ones. Then write the total.

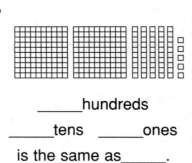

Anyone for a number 21?

1.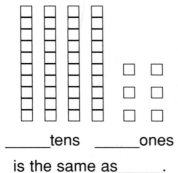

_____tens _____ones

is the same as_____.

2.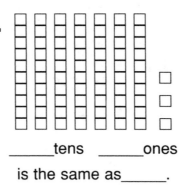

_____tens _____ones

is the same as_____.

3.

_____hundreds

_____tens _____ones

is the same as_____.

Write how many hundreds, tens, and ones.

4. 37 _____tens _____ones

5. 80 _____tens _____ones

6. 513 _____hundreds _____ten _____ones

7. 902 _____hundreds _____tens _____ones

Circle the correct answer.

8. two: 12 20 2 22   **9.** four: 4 14 40 44

10. 9: nine nin ten none   **11.** 6: seven six two sixteen

Circle the number that is <u>more</u>.

12. 32 34 27 43   **13.** 48 44 41 40

14. 818 918 900 920   **15.** 510 570 550 556

Write the missing numbers.

16. 17 ___ 19 ___ 21   **17.** 254 ___ 256 ___ 258

18. ___ 333 ___ 335 ___

Name _____ Date _____

Numeration Assessment
Write how many hundreds, tens, and ones. Then write the total.

1.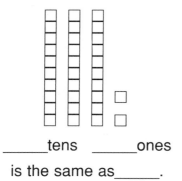

_____tens _____ones

is the same as_____.

2.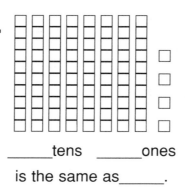

_____tens _____ones

is the same as_____.

3.

_____hundreds

_____tens _____ones

is the same as_____.

Write how many hundreds, tens, and ones.

4. 28 _____tens _____ones

5. 64 _____tens _____ones

6. 408 _____hundreds _____tens _____ones

7. 762 _____hundreds _____tens _____ones

Circle the correct answer.

8. three: 2 3 13 20   **9.** eight: 8 18 80 88

10. 10: two ten three twelve   **11.** 24: seven six twenty-four

Circle the number that is <u>more</u>.

12. 45 54 44 59   **13.** 72 27 39 70

14. 515 550 509 555   **15.** 211 112 212 121

Write the missing numbers.

16. 15 ___ 17 ___ 19   **17.** 176 ___ 178 ___ 180

18. ___ 260 ___ 262 ___

www.summerbridgeactivities.com   Math Connection—Grade 2—RBP3780

Addition Chart

Complete the addition chart.

+	0	1	2	3	4	5	6	7	8	9	10
0	0										
1											
2											
3											
4											
5											
6											
7											
8											
9											
10											

Math Connection—Grade 2—RBP3780   www.summerbridgeactivities.com   ©RBP Books

Addition Facts

Solve the problems. Then answer each question.

It's important to learn your addition facts. Try to learn these tricks.

I'm sure you'll have no problem finishing these problems!

1. What is zero plus any number? _____

3	6	8	9	4
+ 0	+ 0	+ 0	+ 0	+ 0

2. What is one plus any number? _____

4	7	5	2	1
+ 1	+ 1	+ 1	+ 1	+ 1

3. What is ten plus any number? _____

2	6	8	9	5
+ 10	+ 10	+ 10	+ 10	+ 10

4. What is nine plus any number? _____

2	6	8	9	5
+ 9	+ 9	+ 9	+ 9	+ 9

Adding Doubles

 Learning the doubles can help you learn other addition facts. If you know 7 + 7 = 14, then you know 7 + 8 is one more, 15.

Add the doubles.

1. 0 + 0 = ____**0**____   4 + 4 = _____   8 + 8 = _____

1 + 1 = _____   5 + 5 = _____   9 + 9 = _____

2 + 2 = _____   6 + 6 = _____   10 + 10 = _____

3 + 3 = _____   7 + 7 = _____

2. What is the pattern? _____

Practice

3.
$$\begin{array}{r} 9 \\ + 9 \\ \hline \end{array} \qquad \begin{array}{r} 7 \\ + 7 \\ \hline \end{array} \qquad \begin{array}{r} 6 \\ + 6 \\ \hline \end{array} \qquad \begin{array}{r} 2 \\ + 2 \\ \hline \end{array} \qquad \begin{array}{r} 4 \\ + 4 \\ \hline \end{array}$$

4.
$$\begin{array}{r} 8 \\ + 8 \\ \hline \end{array} \qquad \begin{array}{r} 1 \\ + 1 \\ \hline \end{array} \qquad \begin{array}{r} 3 \\ + 3 \\ \hline \end{array} \qquad \begin{array}{r} 10 \\ + 10 \\ \hline \end{array} \qquad \begin{array}{r} 5 \\ + 5 \\ \hline \end{array}$$

Addition Facts 0–10

Solve each problem.

Start at the first number; then count up.
4, 5, 6.
4 plus 2 equals 6.

$$\begin{array}{r} 4 \\ + 2 \\ \hline \mathbf{6} \end{array}$$

1.

$$\begin{array}{r} 1 \\ + 4 \\ \hline \end{array}$$
$$\begin{array}{r} 3 \\ + 1 \\ \hline \end{array}$$
$$\begin{array}{r} 9 \\ + 1 \\ \hline \end{array}$$
$$\begin{array}{r} 3 \\ + 5 \\ \hline \end{array}$$
$$\begin{array}{r} 2 \\ + 5 \\ \hline \end{array}$$

2.

$$\begin{array}{r} 0 \\ + 6 \\ \hline \end{array}$$
$$\begin{array}{r} 2 \\ + 8 \\ \hline \end{array}$$
$$\begin{array}{r} 2 \\ + 3 \\ \hline \end{array}$$
$$\begin{array}{r} 2 \\ + 6 \\ \hline \end{array}$$
$$\begin{array}{r} 4 \\ + 1 \\ \hline \end{array}$$

3.

$$\begin{array}{r} 3 \\ + 4 \\ \hline \end{array}$$
$$\begin{array}{r} 3 \\ + 7 \\ \hline \end{array}$$
$$\begin{array}{r} 0 \\ + 3 \\ \hline \end{array}$$
$$\begin{array}{r} 4 \\ + 5 \\ \hline \end{array}$$
$$\begin{array}{r} 3 \\ + 3 \\ \hline \end{array}$$

4.

$$\begin{array}{r} 3 \\ + 2 \\ \hline \end{array}$$
$$\begin{array}{r} 6 \\ + 3 \\ \hline \end{array}$$
$$\begin{array}{r} 2 \\ + 2 \\ \hline \end{array}$$
$$\begin{array}{r} 1 \\ + 9 \\ \hline \end{array}$$
$$\begin{array}{r} 4 \\ + 6 \\ \hline \end{array}$$

5.

$$\begin{array}{r} 1 \\ + 5 \\ \hline \end{array}$$
$$\begin{array}{r} 3 \\ + 0 \\ \hline \end{array}$$
$$\begin{array}{r} 2 \\ + 4 \\ \hline \end{array}$$
$$\begin{array}{r} 4 \\ + 4 \\ \hline \end{array}$$
$$\begin{array}{r} 5 \\ + 0 \\ \hline \end{array}$$

6.

$$\begin{array}{r} 2 \\ + 0 \\ \hline \end{array}$$
$$\begin{array}{r} 8 \\ + 1 \\ \hline \end{array}$$
$$\begin{array}{r} 4 \\ + 6 \\ \hline \end{array}$$
$$\begin{array}{r} 2 \\ + 7 \\ \hline \end{array}$$
$$\begin{array}{r} 5 \\ + 5 \\ \hline \end{array}$$

Name _____   Date _____

Addition Problem Solving 0–10
Read and solve the problems.

 Sometimes it helps to draw a picture.
Then just count.

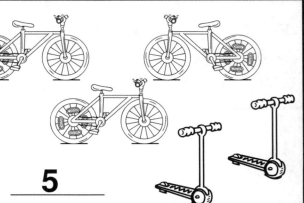

3 boys rode on bikes.

2 boys rode on scooters.

How many boys in all?   __3__ + __2__ = __5__

---

1. Jim rode his bike 3 miles on Monday and 5 miles on Tuesday.

How far did he ride in all?

_____miles

2. There were 6 lions in the first cage and 4 lions in another cage.

How many lions in all?

_____lions

---

3. Six children went swimming.

Three children went for a walk.

How many children were there in all?

_____children

4. Tanner has 7 train cars.

His sister gave him 2 for his birthday.

How many train cars does he have in all?

_____train cars

Math Connection—Grade 2—RBP3780   www.summerbridgeactivities.com   © RBP Books

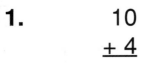

Addition Problem Solving 11–18

Solve each problem.

1.
$$\begin{array}{r} 10 \\ +\ 4 \\ \hline \end{array}$$
$$\begin{array}{r} 7 \\ +\ 8 \\ \hline \end{array}$$
$$\begin{array}{r} 4 \\ +\ 12 \\ \hline \end{array}$$
$$\begin{array}{r} 3 \\ +\ 11 \\ \hline \end{array}$$
$$\begin{array}{r} 5 \\ +\ 8 \\ \hline \end{array}$$

2.
$$\begin{array}{r} 11 \\ +\ 7 \\ \hline \end{array}$$
$$\begin{array}{r} 5 \\ +\ 12 \\ \hline \end{array}$$
$$\begin{array}{r} 3 \\ +\ 13 \\ \hline \end{array}$$
$$\begin{array}{r} 4 \\ +\ 9 \\ \hline \end{array}$$
$$\begin{array}{r} 11 \\ +\ 2 \\ \hline \end{array}$$

3.
$$\begin{array}{r} 8 \\ +\ 9 \\ \hline \end{array}$$
$$\begin{array}{r} 6 \\ +\ 9 \\ \hline \end{array}$$
$$\begin{array}{r} 5 \\ +\ 11 \\ \hline \end{array}$$
$$\begin{array}{r} 6 \\ +\ 8 \\ \hline \end{array}$$
$$\begin{array}{r} 10 \\ +\ 5 \\ \hline \end{array}$$

4.
$$\begin{array}{r} 7 \\ +\ 4 \\ \hline \end{array}$$
$$\begin{array}{r} 10 \\ +\ 6 \\ \hline \end{array}$$
$$\begin{array}{r} 9 \\ +\ 5 \\ \hline \end{array}$$
$$\begin{array}{r} 7 \\ +\ 6 \\ \hline \end{array}$$
$$\begin{array}{r} 5 \\ +\ 6 \\ \hline \end{array}$$

5.
$$\begin{array}{r} 6 \\ +\ 12 \\ \hline \end{array}$$
$$\begin{array}{r} 2 \\ +\ 15 \\ \hline \end{array}$$
$$\begin{array}{r} 10 \\ +\ 3 \\ \hline \end{array}$$
$$\begin{array}{r} 2 \\ +\ 13 \\ \hline \end{array}$$
$$\begin{array}{r} 12 \\ +\ 4 \\ \hline \end{array}$$

6.
$$\begin{array}{r} 14 \\ +\ 4 \\ \hline \end{array}$$
$$\begin{array}{r} 4 \\ +\ 11 \\ \hline \end{array}$$
$$\begin{array}{r} 8 \\ +\ 3 \\ \hline \end{array}$$
$$\begin{array}{r} 7 \\ +\ 9 \\ \hline \end{array}$$
$$\begin{array}{r} 11 \\ +\ 3 \\ \hline \end{array}$$

Addition Problem Solving 11–18

Solve the problems. Do your work in the box. Write your answer on the line.

Andy has 8 toy bears and 4 other toy animals.
How many animals does Andy have altogether?
 Andy has 12 toy animals.

$$\begin{array}{r} 8 \\ + 4 \\ \hline 12 \end{array}$$

 8 plus 4 equals 12. For a story problem, I write my answer like this: Andy has 12 toy animals.

1. Nick ate 6 peanuts and 7 walnuts.

How many nuts did Nick eat?

_____

2. Rachel had 3 pieces of blue bubble gum and 8 pieces of red bubble gum.

How many pieces of bubble gum did Rachel have?

_____

3. Josh has 4 green train cars and 9 blue train cars.

How many train cars does Josh have altogether?

_____

4. Nate played 5 minutes the first half of the game and 9 minutes the second half.

How many minutes did Nate play?

_____

5. Mrs. White has 7 striped cats and 8 gray cats.

How many cats does she have altogether?

_____

6. Jeff has 9 oranges and 8 apples left to sell.

How many pieces of fruit does Jeff have to sell?

_____

Math Connection—Grade 2—RBP3780   www.summerbridgeactivities.com   ©RBP Books

Number Families

Complete each equation.

Learning number families will help you learn the addition and subtraction facts.

1.

(7 / 2 5)

__2__ + __5__ = __7__
____ + ____ = ____
____ − ____ = ____
____ − ____ = ____

2.

(8 / 2 10)

____ + ____ = ____
____ + ____ = ____
____ − ____ = ____
____ − ____ = ____

3.

(2 / 6 4)

____ + ____ = ____
____ + ____ = ____
____ − ____ = ____
____ − ____ = ____

4.

(8 / 3 11)

____ + ____ = ____
____ + ____ = ____
____ − ____ = ____
____ − ____ = ____

5.

(8 / 5 13)

____ + ____ = ____
____ + ____ = ____
____ − ____ = ____
____ − ____ = ____

6.

(3 / 10 7)

____ + ____ = ____
____ + ____ = ____
____ − ____ = ____
____ − ____ = ____

7.

(11 / 7 4)

____ + ____ = ____
____ + ____ = ____
____ − ____ = ____
____ − ____ = ____

8.

(9 / 6 3)

____ + ____ = ____
____ + ____ = ____
____ − ____ = ____
____ − ____ = ____

www.summerbridgeactivities.com
Math Connection—Grade 2—RBP3780

Number Families

Complete each equation.

 Picture these groups of numbers in your head. This will help you learn your facts.

1.

$\begin{array}{c} 4 \\ 5 \quad 9 \end{array}$

_____ + _____ = _____
_____ + _____ = _____
_____ − _____ = _____
_____ − _____ = _____

2.

$\begin{array}{c} 7 \\ 3 \quad 10 \end{array}$

_____ + _____ = _____
_____ + _____ = _____
_____ − _____ = _____
_____ − _____ = _____

3.

$\begin{array}{c} 7 \\ 6 \quad 13 \end{array}$

_____ + _____ = _____
_____ + _____ = _____
_____ − _____ = _____
_____ − _____ = _____

4.

$\begin{array}{c} 7 \\ 8 \quad 15 \end{array}$

_____ + _____ = _____
_____ + _____ = _____
_____ − _____ = _____
_____ − _____ = _____

5.

$\begin{array}{c} 2 \\ 6 \quad 8 \end{array}$

_____ + _____ = _____
_____ + _____ = _____
_____ − _____ = _____
_____ − _____ = _____

6.

$\begin{array}{c} 8 \\ 9 \quad 17 \end{array}$

_____ + _____ = _____
_____ + _____ = _____
_____ − _____ = _____
_____ − _____ = _____

7.

$\begin{array}{c} 6 \\ 8 \quad 14 \end{array}$

_____ + _____ = _____
_____ + _____ = _____
_____ − _____ = _____
_____ − _____ = _____

8.

$\begin{array}{c} 5 \\ 7 \quad 12 \end{array}$

_____ + _____ = _____
_____ + _____ = _____
_____ − _____ = _____
_____ − _____ = _____

Math Connection—Grade 2—RBP3780   www.summerbridgeactivities.com   © RBP Books

Subtraction Facts 0–10
Solve each problem.

Start at the first number; then count back.
7, 6, 5.
7 minus 2 equals 5.

$$\begin{array}{r} 7 \\ -\,2 \\ \hline \mathbf{5} \end{array}$$

1.

10	4	6	9	8
− 1	− 4	− 0	− 6	− 2

2.

5	2	5	10	7
− 4	− 1	− 2	− 4	− 3

3.

10	7	6	9	10
− 8	− 2	− 3	− 3	− 6

4.

6	1	5	2	5
− 2	− 0	− 4	− 2	− 3

5.

9	10	7	6	8
− 1	− 5	− 4	− 6	− 0

6.

7	4	10	6	3
− 7	− 3	− 3	− 4	− 3

RBP Books   www.summerbridgeactivities.com   Math Connection—Grade 2—RBP3780

Subtraction Problem Solving 0–10

Read and solve the problems.

 Cross off the number talked about.
Then count the rest.

Mike has 10 goldfish.

3 are eating.

How many goldfish are not eating?

$$\begin{array}{r} 10 \\ -\ 3 \\ \hline \mathbf{7} \end{array}$$

---

1. Nine children were skating.

Two children fell down.

How many children did not fall down?

_____

2. Jack had 8 model cars.

He gave 2 to his brother.

How many cars does Jack have left?

_____

3. Eli checked out 6 books from the library.

He read 3 books.

How many more books does he have to read?

_____

4. Nate is 7 years old.

His sister is 4 years old.

How much older is Nate than his sister?

_____

Math Connection—Grade 2—RBP3780   www.summerbridgeactivities.com   ©RBP Books

Subtraction Problem Solving 11–18

Solve each problem.

Think about the number families.
Try to learn these facts.

1. $\begin{array}{r} 15 \\ -\ 8 \\ \hline \end{array}$	$\begin{array}{r} 13 \\ -\ 7 \\ \hline \end{array}$	$\begin{array}{r} 16 \\ -\ 4 \\ \hline \end{array}$	$\begin{array}{r} 18 \\ -\ 18 \\ \hline \end{array}$	$\begin{array}{r} 17 \\ -\ 6 \\ \hline \end{array}$
2. $\begin{array}{r} 14 \\ -\ 8 \\ \hline \end{array}$	$\begin{array}{r} 16 \\ -\ 2 \\ \hline \end{array}$	$\begin{array}{r} 14 \\ -\ 7 \\ \hline \end{array}$	$\begin{array}{r} 13 \\ -\ 9 \\ \hline \end{array}$	$\begin{array}{r} 18 \\ -\ 5 \\ \hline \end{array}$
3. $\begin{array}{r} 11 \\ -\ 6 \\ \hline \end{array}$	$\begin{array}{r} 16 \\ -\ 10 \\ \hline \end{array}$	$\begin{array}{r} 14 \\ -\ 3 \\ \hline \end{array}$	$\begin{array}{r} 17 \\ -\ 10 \\ \hline \end{array}$	$\begin{array}{r} 11 \\ -\ 4 \\ \hline \end{array}$
4. $\begin{array}{r} 16 \\ -\ 7 \\ \hline \end{array}$	$\begin{array}{r} 13 \\ -\ 2 \\ \hline \end{array}$	$\begin{array}{r} 12 \\ -\ 7 \\ \hline \end{array}$	$\begin{array}{r} 14 \\ -\ 5 \\ \hline \end{array}$	$\begin{array}{r} 15 \\ -\ 12 \\ \hline \end{array}$
5. $\begin{array}{r} 18 \\ -\ 1 \\ \hline \end{array}$	$\begin{array}{r} 14 \\ -\ 9 \\ \hline \end{array}$	$\begin{array}{r} 16 \\ -\ 3 \\ \hline \end{array}$	$\begin{array}{r} 17 \\ -\ 8 \\ \hline \end{array}$	$\begin{array}{r} 12 \\ -\ 8 \\ \hline \end{array}$
6. $\begin{array}{r} 15 \\ -\ 13 \\ \hline \end{array}$	$\begin{array}{r} 13 \\ -\ 6 \\ \hline \end{array}$	$\begin{array}{r} 18 \\ -\ 7 \\ \hline \end{array}$	$\begin{array}{r} 15 \\ -\ 9 \\ \hline \end{array}$	$\begin{array}{r} 12 \\ -\ 9 \\ \hline \end{array}$

Subtraction Problem Solving 11–18

Solve the problems. Do your work in the box. Write your answer on the line.

My sister has 15 dolls. She is playing with 7 dolls. How many dolls is she not playing with?	$\begin{array}{r} 15 \\ -\,7 \\ \hline \mathbf{8} \end{array}$

 15 take away 7 equals 8. I write the answer. <u>She is not playing with 8 dolls.</u>

1. Dan's dog had 13 puppies.

He gave 9 of the puppies away.

How many puppies did Dan keep?

_____

2. Max had 18 marbles.

He lost 9 in the game.

How many marbles does he have left?

_____

3. Jane has 12 dresses.

7 of the dresses do not fit anymore.

How many dresses can Jane still wear?

_____

4. Cowboy Jim had 17 cows.

He sold 8.

How many cows does he have left?

_____

5. Mother had 13 pieces of mail.

She has opened 6 pieces of mail.

How many pieces of mail does she have left to open?

_____

6. Gina had 11 hair ribbons.

She can only find 8 ribbons.

How many hair ribbons has she lost?

_____

Math Connection—Grade 2—RBP3780   www.summerbridgeactivities.com   ©RBP Books

Addition and Subtraction Practice 0–10.

Solve each problem.

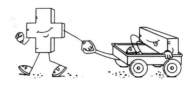

 Watch the signs!

1.
$$\begin{array}{r} 3 \\ +\,0 \\ \hline \end{array}$$
$$\begin{array}{r} 6 \\ -\,3 \\ \hline \end{array}$$
$$\begin{array}{r} 2 \\ +\,8 \\ \hline \end{array}$$
$$\begin{array}{r} 3 \\ -\,2 \\ \hline \end{array}$$
$$\begin{array}{r} 4 \\ -\,2 \\ \hline \end{array}$$

2.
$$\begin{array}{r} 10 \\ -\,5 \\ \hline \end{array}$$
$$\begin{array}{r} 2 \\ +\,2 \\ \hline \end{array}$$
$$\begin{array}{r} 6 \\ +\,2 \\ \hline \end{array}$$
$$\begin{array}{r} 9 \\ -\,8 \\ \hline \end{array}$$
$$\begin{array}{r} 5 \\ -\,4 \\ \hline \end{array}$$

3.
$$\begin{array}{r} 6 \\ +\,4 \\ \hline \end{array}$$
$$\begin{array}{r} 2 \\ +\,1 \\ \hline \end{array}$$
$$\begin{array}{r} 2 \\ -\,2 \\ \hline \end{array}$$
$$\begin{array}{r} 9 \\ -\,4 \\ \hline \end{array}$$
$$\begin{array}{r} 6 \\ -\,5 \\ \hline \end{array}$$

4.
$$\begin{array}{r} 7 \\ -\,4 \\ \hline \end{array}$$
$$\begin{array}{r} 7 \\ +\,0 \\ \hline \end{array}$$
$$\begin{array}{r} 10 \\ -\,8 \\ \hline \end{array}$$
$$\begin{array}{r} 4 \\ -\,4 \\ \hline \end{array}$$
$$\begin{array}{r} 3 \\ +\,2 \\ \hline \end{array}$$

5.
$$\begin{array}{r} 8 \\ +\,1 \\ \hline \end{array}$$
$$\begin{array}{r} 6 \\ -\,2 \\ \hline \end{array}$$
$$\begin{array}{r} 4 \\ -\,1 \\ \hline \end{array}$$
$$\begin{array}{r} 1 \\ +\,5 \\ \hline \end{array}$$
$$\begin{array}{r} 7 \\ +\,3 \\ \hline \end{array}$$

6.
$$\begin{array}{r} 9 \\ -\,7 \\ \hline \end{array}$$
$$\begin{array}{r} 8 \\ +\,2 \\ \hline \end{array}$$
$$\begin{array}{r} 1 \\ +\,9 \\ \hline \end{array}$$
$$\begin{array}{r} 10 \\ -\,10 \\ \hline \end{array}$$
$$\begin{array}{r} 8 \\ -\,6 \\ \hline \end{array}$$

Addition and Subtraction Problem Solving 0–10

Read and solve the problems.

Draw a picture to help you
think through each problem.

1. Betty planted 5 roses in her flower
garden.

Three roses were red.

The rest of them were pink.

How many roses were pink?

_____

2. My aunt has 8 black cats and 3
gray ones.

How many cats does she have in
all?

_____

3. Craig bought 2 erasers and 7
pencils for school.

How many things did he buy in all?

_____

4. Ten nuts were on the ground.

The chipmunks ate 7 of them.

How many nuts were left on the
ground?

_____

5. Carla has 10 crayons.

Six of them are broken.

How many crayons are not
broken?

_____

6. A rabbit ate 6 carrots in one day
and 3 the next day.

How many carrots did the rabbit
eat in all?

_____

Addition and Subtraction Practice 11–18

Solve each problem.

Watch the signs.
Keep practicing until you know these facts.

I love math this much!

1.

1	16	6	4	15	10
+ 8	− 6	+ 6	+ 11	+ 1	+ 3

2.

5	3	18	9	16	11
+ 8	+ 11	− 9	+ 5	− 7	+ 7

3.

17	7	11	7	12	14
− 9	+ 5	+ 4	+ 6	− 7	− 9

4.

18	11	8	16	14	13
− 4	− 3	+ 8	− 9	− 5	+ 5

5.

14	15	8	16	6	15
+ 4	− 12	+ 9	− 8	+ 9	− 9

6.

7	9	5	16	16	2
+ 7	+ 9	+ 6	− 7	− 0	+ 16

RBP Books   www.summerbridgeactivities.com   Math Connection—Grade 2—RBP3780

Addition and Subtraction Practice
Solve each problem.

1. 5   7   6   5   10   3
      +5   +8   +7   +8   +4   +8

2. 4   8   10   9   7   6
      +7   +6   +7   +3   +2   +5

3. 10   5   7   4   6   7
      +3   +7   +3   +9   +7   +9

4. 12   10   17   13   14   15
      −4   −7   −9   −7   −8   −6

5. 15   14   12   10   11   12
      −7   −7   −5   −3   −6   −9

6. 16   13   14   11   10   12
      −8   −5   −9   −7   −4   −6

Math Connection—Grade 2—RBP3780   www.summerbridgeactivities.com   ©RBP Books

Addition and Subtraction Problem Solving 11–18

Solve the problems. Do your work in the box. Write your answer on the line.

Stan has 15 pets. He has 6 cats. How many pets are not cats?	$$\begin{array}{r} 15 \\ -\ 6 \\ \hline 9 \end{array}$$

 15 pets total.
 I subtract 6 because those are cats.
 I write <u>9 are not cats.</u>

1. Pat has 6 cats and 8 goldfish.

How many pets does
Pat have?

2. The dog had 11 bones.

He buried 7 of them.

How many bones does the
dog have left?

3. Josie ran for 6 minutes the first day
and 8 minutes the second day.

How many minutes did
Josie run?

4. Brock had 15 special jars.

Six broke.

How many jars does Brock
have left?

5. Chan had 12 cookies.

He ate 5 of the cookies.

How many does he
have left?

6. Mary picked 4 apples from
one tree and 9 apples from another
tree.

How many apples did
Mary pick?

Addition and Subtraction Facts Assessment

Solve the problems.

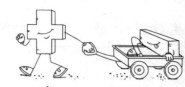

1.
$$\begin{array}{r} 8 \\ +7 \\ \hline \end{array}\qquad \begin{array}{r} 4 \\ +6 \\ \hline \end{array}\qquad \begin{array}{r} 3 \\ +9 \\ \hline \end{array}\qquad \begin{array}{r} 7 \\ +2 \\ \hline \end{array}\qquad \begin{array}{r} 1 \\ +10 \\ \hline \end{array}\qquad \begin{array}{r} 6 \\ +6 \\ \hline \end{array}$$

2.
$$\begin{array}{r} 7 \\ +4 \\ \hline \end{array}\qquad \begin{array}{r} 5 \\ +5 \\ \hline \end{array}\qquad \begin{array}{r} 8 \\ +6 \\ \hline \end{array}\qquad \begin{array}{r} 4 \\ +4 \\ \hline \end{array}\qquad \begin{array}{r} 5 \\ +7 \\ \hline \end{array}\qquad \begin{array}{r} 3 \\ +9 \\ \hline \end{array}$$

3.
$$\begin{array}{r} 9 \\ +9 \\ \hline \end{array}\qquad \begin{array}{r} 7 \\ +6 \\ \hline \end{array}\qquad \begin{array}{r} 5 \\ +8 \\ \hline \end{array}\qquad \begin{array}{r} 2 \\ +9 \\ \hline \end{array}\qquad \begin{array}{r} 8 \\ +8 \\ \hline \end{array}\qquad \begin{array}{r} 6 \\ +5 \\ \hline \end{array}$$

4.
$$\begin{array}{r} 14 \\ -7 \\ \hline \end{array}\qquad \begin{array}{r} 15 \\ -9 \\ \hline \end{array}\qquad \begin{array}{r} 17 \\ -8 \\ \hline \end{array}\qquad \begin{array}{r} 16 \\ -9 \\ \hline \end{array}\qquad \begin{array}{r} 12 \\ -7 \\ \hline \end{array}\qquad \begin{array}{r} 13 \\ -9 \\ \hline \end{array}$$

5.
$$\begin{array}{r} 18 \\ -9 \\ \hline \end{array}\qquad \begin{array}{r} 16 \\ -8 \\ \hline \end{array}\qquad \begin{array}{r} 15 \\ -7 \\ \hline \end{array}\qquad \begin{array}{r} 14 \\ -5 \\ \hline \end{array}\qquad \begin{array}{r} 13 \\ -5 \\ \hline \end{array}\qquad \begin{array}{r} 12 \\ -8 \\ \hline \end{array}$$

6.
$$\begin{array}{r} 15 \\ -10 \\ \hline \end{array}\qquad \begin{array}{r} 13 \\ -7 \\ \hline \end{array}\qquad \begin{array}{r} 11 \\ -7 \\ \hline \end{array}\qquad \begin{array}{r} 12 \\ -4 \\ \hline \end{array}\qquad \begin{array}{r} 16 \\ -6 \\ \hline \end{array}\qquad \begin{array}{r} 12 \\ -6 \\ \hline \end{array}$$

Math Connection—Grade 2—RBP3780   www.summerbridgeactivities.com   ©RBP Books

Addition and Subtraction Facts Assessment

Solve the problems.

I bet you can do these problems in a snap!

1.
$$6 + 7$$ $$5 + 6$$ $$2 + 9$$ $$7 + 4$$ $$8 + 10$$ $$8 + 3$$

2.
$$7 + 3$$ $$7 + 5$$ $$9 + 6$$ $$8 + 4$$ $$8 + 6$$ $$8 + 9$$

3.
$$6 + 9$$ $$6 + 6$$ $$7 + 8$$ $$5 + 9$$ $$7 + 10$$ $$4 + 5$$

4.
$$10 - 7$$ $$14 - 9$$ $$13 - 8$$ $$17 - 9$$ $$11 - 7$$ $$12 - 9$$

5.
$$15 - 9$$ $$16 - 9$$ $$18 - 8$$ $$14 - 6$$ $$13 - 7$$ $$12 - 6$$

6.
$$14 - 7$$ $$12 - 8$$ $$11 - 5$$ $$12 - 4$$ $$15 - 8$$ $$13 - 9$$

Skip Counting with Money
Write how much.

 penny = 1¢   nickel = 5¢   dime = 10¢

1. Count the pennies by 2s.

[____] ¢ (pennies rows)

2. Count the nickels by 5s.

[____] ¢

3. Count the dimes by 10s.

[____] ¢

Counting Coins
Count the coins. Write how much.

 + = 50¢ + = 75¢

25¢   25¢   25¢

 equals 2 dimes, 1 nickel

 equals 5 nickels

 equals 25 pennies

1.

_____ ¢

2.

_____ ¢

3.

_____ ¢

4.

_____ ¢

5.

_____ ¢

6.

_____ ¢

Counting Coins
Count the coins. Write how much.

50¢　　　equals
2 quarters　　　equals
5 dimes　　　equals
10 nickels

1.

_____ ¢

2.

_____ ¢

3.

_____ ¢

4.

_____ ¢

5.

_____ ¢

6.

_____ ¢

Math Connection—Grade 2—RBP3780　　www.summerbridgeactivities.com　　©RBP Books

Money Practice

On the line next to each toy, write the letter that stands for the amount of money that each toy costs.

 I start with the quarter, which is 25¢. Then I add the dime, which makes 35¢. Then I add the two pennies to make 37¢.  37¢ **37¢**

A.

B.

C.

D.

E.

F.

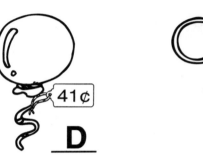 41¢

90¢

D

72¢

58¢

_____

77¢

_____   63¢

© RBP Books   www.summerbridgeactivities.com   Math Connection—Grade 2—RBP3780

Money Practice

Fill in the number of coins needed to make the correct amount. Use the fewest coins possible.

To make 73¢, I need 1 half-dollar.
That's 50¢. Then 2 dimes.
That's 60, 70¢. Then 3 pennies.

	Half-dollar	Quarter	Dime	Nickel	Penny
1. 73¢	1		2		3
2. 84¢					
3. 91¢					
4. 51¢					
5. 39¢					
6. 22¢					
7. 43¢					
8. 69¢					
9. 45¢					
10. 62¢					

Counting Money

Count the money. Write how much.

$1.00

$1.00

$1.00

$1.00

1.

_____

2.

_____

3.

_____

4.

_____

5.

_____

6.

_____

Money Practice

Circle the exact amount of money needed to buy each item.

 Remember to use skip counting when counting money.

 I'm saving my money for summer vacation!

1.

2.

3.

$82¢$

4.

Math Connection—Grade 2—RBP3780   www.summerbridgeactivities.com   © RBP Books

Problem Solving with Money

Solve each problem.

Zach has 3 quarters.

Does he have enough to buy a book for 80¢?

He has __**75¢**__.

Three quarters equals 75¢. No, that's not enough to buy the coloring book.

Yes   (No)

---

1. Tom has 2 quarters and 1 dime.

Does he have enough money to buy a toy truck that costs 75¢?

He has _____¢.

Yes   No

2. Jane has 3 dimes and 4 nickels.

Does she have enough to buy a toy that costs 25¢?

She has _____¢.

Yes   No

---

3. Mom gave Denise 3 quarters and 2 dimes to buy milk. Milk costs 92¢ a quart. Does Denise have enough to buy a quart of milk?

She has _____¢.

Yes   No

4. Tanner has 2 dimes, 1 nickel, and 4 pennies.

Does he have enough to buy a toy train that costs 46¢?

He has _____¢.

Yes   No

---

5. If you had 1 half-dollar and 3 dimes, could you buy a kite that costs 95¢?

You have _____¢.

Yes   No

6. Grayson has 8 nickels and 9 pennies.

Does he have enough to buy a notebook that costs 50¢?

He has _____¢.

Yes   No

---

www.summerbridgeactivities.com   **Math Connection—Grade 2—RBP3780**

Telling Time: Clock Questions

Use this clock to answer the questions.

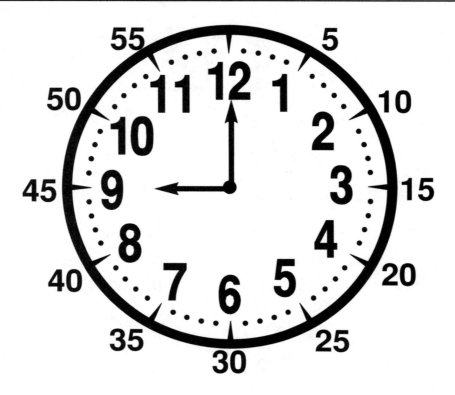

1. What time does the clock show? _____.

2. The long hand is called the _____ hand.

3. What is the short hand called? _____

4. How many minutes are there from one number to the next? _____

5. How many minutes are in an hour? _____

6. How many hours are on the clock? _____

7. How many minutes are in a half hour? _____

8. How many hours are in a day? _____

Telling Time to the Hour and Half Hour

Circle the time shown on each clock.

The short hand is called the hour hand. It tells the hour.
The long hand is the minute hand. It tells the minutes.
This clock shows 30 minutes past 9 o'clock. It shows 9:30.

1.

(3:00)   3:30   12:00

2.

2:30   3:30   1:30

3.

7:00   7:30   8:30

4.

6:00   12:30   12:00

5.

11:00   12:00   10:00

6.

12:00   12:30   6:00

© RBP Books   www.summerbridgeactivities.com   Math Connection—Grade 2—RBP3780

Telling Time to the Hour and Half Hour

Draw hands on each clock to show the time listed in each problem.

Remember to make the hour hand short and the minute hand longer.

 Time to draw clock hands!

1.

4:00

2.

7:30

3.

11:30

4.

10:30

5.

2:00

6.

3:30

Telling Time: Writing Time

Write the time shown on these clocks.

 Remember there are 5 minutes between each number.
Count by 5s to find the minutes.

Time to write time!

1.

$\underline{2}$: $\underline{15}$

2.

_____ : _____

3.

_____ : _____

4.

_____ : _____

5.

_____ : _____

6.

_____ : _____

www.summerbridgeactivities.com   **Math Connection—Grade 2—RBP3780**

Telling Time: Drawing Clock Hands

Draw hands on each clock to show the time listed in each problem.

 Draw the hour hand first.
Then count by 5s to draw
the minute hand.

 Tooth-hurty is the best time to see a dentist!

1.

6:05

2.

9:35

3.

1:15

4.

2:40

5.

11:20

6.

3:55

Problem Solving with Time

Read and solve the problems.

Nick leaves on the bus for school at 8:00. The bus ride takes 20 minutes. What time does Nick get to school?

Eight o'clock plus 20 minutes. Nick gets to school at 8:20.

1. The children have a snack at 10:00.

They eat lunch 2 hours later.

What time do the children eat lunch?

2. The class has silent reading every morning at 9:00.

They read for 15 minutes.

What time are they finished with silent reading?

3. Recess lasts 10 minutes.

It starts at 2:00.

What time does it end?

4. Ben leaves school at 3:30.

He rides the bus for 15 minutes.

What time does he get off the bus?

5. Liz begins her homework at 4:00.

She finishes at 4:30.

How many minutes does Liz work on her homework?

6. Justin studies his spelling words for 10 minutes.

He starts studying at 4:05.

What time does Justin finish?

Name _____ Date _____

Money and Time Assessment
Count the coins. Write how much.

1.

2.

3.

4.
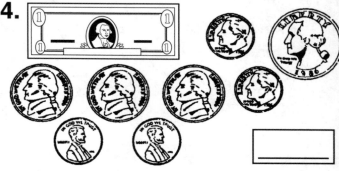

Write the time shown on the clocks.

5.

_____ : _____

6.

_____ : _____

7.

_____ : _____

8.

_____ : _____

Math Connection—Grade 2—RBP3780   www.summerbridgeactivities.com   ©RBP Books

Money and Time Assessment

Count the coins. Write how much.

1.

2.

3.

4.

Write the time shown on the clocks.

5.

_____ : _____

6.

_____ : _____

7.

_____ : _____

8.

_____ : _____

© RBP Books   www.summerbridgeactivities.com   Math Connection—Grade 2—RBP3780

Column Addition
Solve each problem.

 Add the first two numbers. Then add the sum of the first two to the last number. 4 plus 2 equals 6. 6 plus 5 equals 11.	4 2 + 5 **11**

1.

5	2	8	6	4
1	2	8	5	4
+ 8	+ 3	+ 2	+ 1	+ 4

2.

7	3	10	6	5
2	6	3	4	8
+ 3	+ 9	+ 3	+ 6	+ 4

3.

3	4	3	1	5
2	3	3	9	7
+ 3	+ 5	+ 3	+ 8	+ 6

4.

9	6	6	4	5
2	4	7	6	3
5	2	2	3	2
+ 2	+ 6	+ 4	+ 7	+ 5

Math Connection—Grade 2—RBP3780

www.summerbridgeactivities.com

Name _____ Date _____

Column Addition Problem Solving

Solve the problems. Do your work in the box. Write your answer on the line.

 Remember to add the sum of the first two numbers to the third number.

1. Max caught 4 worms, Jack caught 6 worms, and Len caught 9 worms.

How many worms did the boys catch altogether?

2. Kristi picked 13 ears of corn, Jess picked 11 ears of corn, and Ashley picked 20 ears of corn.

How many ears of corn did the girls pick?

3. Kathy has 7 dogs.
Keith has 6 dogs.
Andy has 4 dogs.

How many dogs do they have altogether?

4. Six people left the party at 9:00.
Eleven people left at 9:30.
Twelve people left at 10:00.

How many people left the party?

5. Nina brought 23 buttons, Nick brought 14 buttons, and
Ed brought 31 buttons.

How many buttons did they have altogether?

6. Brad has 14 pencils that are not sharpened, 11 sharpened pencils, and 21 colored pencils.

How many pencils does Brad have altogether?

2-Digit Addition
Solve each problem.

Add the ones first.
5 plus 3 equals 8.

```
 2 5
+1 3
   8
```

Then add the tens.
2 plus 1 equals 3.

```
 2 5
+1 3
 3 8
```

```
 2 5
+1 3
 3 8
```

1.
```
  24      16      32      16      19
+ 11    + 12    + 21    + 23    + 20
```

2.
```
  18      12      26      24      45
+ 11    + 44    + 70    + 51    + 40
```

3.
```
  17      23      73       7      25
+ 52    + 43    + 24    + 12    + 14
```

4.
```
  13      10      44      21      62
+ 15    + 29    + 40    + 14    + 30
```

5.
```
  25      22      11       4      36
+ 10    + 22    + 24    + 14    + 11
```

6.
```
  10      14      62      41      66
+ 10    + 82    + 37    +  8    + 33
```

Math Connection—Grade 2—RBP3780   www.summerbridgeactivities.com ©RBP Books

Name _____ Date _____

2-Digit Addition
Solve each problem.

 Remember to add the ones first.
Then add the tens.

1.
$$12 + 13$$ $$24 + 15$$ $$34 + 22$$ $$19 + 70$$ $$55 + 22$$

2.
$$31 + 27$$ $$27 + 30$$ $$81 + 17$$ $$77 + 12$$ $$33 + 26$$

3.
$$15 + 42$$ $$40 + 28$$ $$22 + 24$$ $$41 + 27$$ $$63 + 34$$

4.
$$27 + 50$$ $$31 + 58$$ $$54 + 14$$ $$17 + 70$$ $$33 + 11$$

5.
$$36 + 22$$ $$51 + 28$$ $$70 + 29$$ $$28 + 21$$ $$61 + 17$$

6.
$$33 + 61$$ $$42 + 32$$ $$53 + 32$$ $$18 + 20$$ $$31 + 41$$

2-Digit Subtraction

Solve each problem.

Subtract the ones first.
5 minus 4 equals 1.

$$\begin{array}{r} 3\,|\,5 \\ -\,2\,|\,4 \\ \hline 1 \end{array}$$

Then subtract the tens.
3 minus 2 equals 1.

$$\begin{array}{r} 3\,|\,5 \\ -\,2\,|\,4 \\ \hline 1\;1 \end{array}$$

$$\begin{array}{r} 3\,5 \\ -\,2\,4 \\ \hline 1\,1 \end{array}$$

1.
$$\begin{array}{r} 24 \\ -\,14 \\ \hline \end{array}$$
$$\begin{array}{r} 64 \\ -\,24 \\ \hline \end{array}$$
$$\begin{array}{r} 83 \\ -\,32 \\ \hline \end{array}$$
$$\begin{array}{r} 46 \\ -\,15 \\ \hline \end{array}$$
$$\begin{array}{r} 87 \\ -\,32 \\ \hline \end{array}$$

2.
$$\begin{array}{r} 98 \\ -\,84 \\ \hline \end{array}$$
$$\begin{array}{r} 32 \\ -\,12 \\ \hline \end{array}$$
$$\begin{array}{r} 57 \\ -\,34 \\ \hline \end{array}$$
$$\begin{array}{r} 75 \\ -\,62 \\ \hline \end{array}$$
$$\begin{array}{r} 29 \\ -\,19 \\ \hline \end{array}$$

3.
$$\begin{array}{r} 59 \\ -\,53 \\ \hline \end{array}$$
$$\begin{array}{r} 18 \\ -\,2 \\ \hline \end{array}$$
$$\begin{array}{r} 80 \\ -\,30 \\ \hline \end{array}$$
$$\begin{array}{r} 37 \\ -\,14 \\ \hline \end{array}$$
$$\begin{array}{r} 66 \\ -\,22 \\ \hline \end{array}$$

4.
$$\begin{array}{r} 27 \\ -\,24 \\ \hline \end{array}$$
$$\begin{array}{r} 72 \\ -\,21 \\ \hline \end{array}$$
$$\begin{array}{r} 33 \\ -\,20 \\ \hline \end{array}$$
$$\begin{array}{r} 45 \\ -\,5 \\ \hline \end{array}$$
$$\begin{array}{r} 39 \\ -\,17 \\ \hline \end{array}$$

5.
$$\begin{array}{r} 39 \\ -\,38 \\ \hline \end{array}$$
$$\begin{array}{r} 50 \\ -\,40 \\ \hline \end{array}$$
$$\begin{array}{r} 77 \\ -\,25 \\ \hline \end{array}$$
$$\begin{array}{r} 81 \\ -\,30 \\ \hline \end{array}$$
$$\begin{array}{r} 28 \\ -\,12 \\ \hline \end{array}$$

6.
$$\begin{array}{r} 94 \\ -\,82 \\ \hline \end{array}$$
$$\begin{array}{r} 63 \\ -\,43 \\ \hline \end{array}$$
$$\begin{array}{r} 36 \\ -\,34 \\ \hline \end{array}$$
$$\begin{array}{r} 10 \\ -\,5 \\ \hline \end{array}$$
$$\begin{array}{r} 47 \\ -\,16 \\ \hline \end{array}$$

Math Connection—Grade 2—RBP3780   www.summerbridgeactivities.com   © RBP Books

2-Digit Subtraction

Solve each problem.

Remember to subtract the ones first.
Then subtract the tens.

1.	58 − 12	35 − 22	92 − 71	78 − 35	52 − 21
2.	67 − 33	84 − 31	96 − 35	88 − 46	79 − 26
3.	68 − 25	58 − 27	62 − 41	97 − 42	74 − 53
4.	55 − 32	68 − 42	56 − 41	85 − 32	76 − 56
5.	79 − 51	48 − 17	66 − 41	95 − 34	86 − 51
6.	61 − 30	74 − 31	82 − 61	94 − 70	59 − 28

2-Digit Addition and Subtraction Practice

Solve each problem.

Watch the signs!
Remember to start with the ones.

Good job! You didn't even have to take off your shoes!

1.

78	36	85	17	84
− 14	+ 21	+ 11	+ 12	− 42

2.

20	75	60	95	84
+ 20	+ 22	+ 30	− 41	− 62

3.

16	38	72	55	25
+ 3	− 25	+ 27	− 24	+ 44

4.

75	10	20	18	62
− 54	+ 10	− 10	+ 21	− 51

5.

47	66	15	82	57
− 24	− 32	+ 1	+ 17	− 36

6.

62	81	77	94	14
− 60	+18	− 33	− 54	+ 13

Math Connection—Grade 2—RBP3780

© RBP Books

2-Digit Addition and Subtraction Practice

Solve each problem.

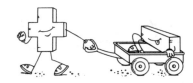

Knowing your basic facts makes even hard math easy!

1.

$$
\begin{array}{r} 22 \\ + 16 \\ \hline \end{array}
\quad
\begin{array}{r} 44 \\ + 31 \\ \hline \end{array}
\quad
\begin{array}{r} 61 \\ + 36 \\ \hline \end{array}
\quad
\begin{array}{r} 52 \\ + 27 \\ \hline \end{array}
\quad
\begin{array}{r} 64 \\ + 25 \\ \hline \end{array}
$$

2.

$$
\begin{array}{r} 75 \\ + 21 \\ \hline \end{array}
\quad
\begin{array}{r} 26 \\ + 53 \\ \hline \end{array}
\quad
\begin{array}{r} 30 \\ + 29 \\ \hline \end{array}
\quad
\begin{array}{r} 34 \\ + 51 \\ \hline \end{array}
\quad
\begin{array}{r} 63 \\ + 25 \\ \hline \end{array}
$$

3.

$$
\begin{array}{r} 19 \\ + 80 \\ \hline \end{array}
\quad
\begin{array}{r} 22 \\ + 63 \\ \hline \end{array}
\quad
\begin{array}{r} 32 \\ + 52 \\ \hline \end{array}
\quad
\begin{array}{r} 41 \\ + 46 \\ \hline \end{array}
\quad
\begin{array}{r} 27 \\ + 32 \\ \hline \end{array}
$$

4.

$$
\begin{array}{r} 28 \\ - 16 \\ \hline \end{array}
\quad
\begin{array}{r} 98 \\ - 32 \\ \hline \end{array}
\quad
\begin{array}{r} 87 \\ - 56 \\ \hline \end{array}
\quad
\begin{array}{r} 78 \\ - 17 \\ \hline \end{array}
\quad
\begin{array}{r} 84 \\ - 42 \\ \hline \end{array}
$$

5.

$$
\begin{array}{r} 67 \\ - 21 \\ \hline \end{array}
\quad
\begin{array}{r} 57 \\ - 35 \\ \hline \end{array}
\quad
\begin{array}{r} 66 \\ - 34 \\ \hline \end{array}
\quad
\begin{array}{r} 79 \\ - 37 \\ \hline \end{array}
\quad
\begin{array}{r} 68 \\ - 42 \\ \hline \end{array}
$$

6.

$$
\begin{array}{r} 62 \\ - 41 \\ \hline \end{array}
\quad
\begin{array}{r} 57 \\ - 41 \\ \hline \end{array}
\quad
\begin{array}{r} 88 \\ - 36 \\ \hline \end{array}
\quad
\begin{array}{r} 99 \\ - 76 \\ \hline \end{array}
\quad
\begin{array}{r} 84 \\ - 52 \\ \hline \end{array}
$$

2-Digit Addition and Subtraction Problem Solving

Solve the problems. Do your work in the box. Write your answer on the line.

Do you add or subtract?
Look for these key words
to help you decide.

Add	**Subtract**
in all	left
altogether	more than

1. Thirty-five children are in first grade.

Thirty-three children are in second grade.

How many children are there altogether?

_____

2. There were 75 seats in the theater.

Sixty-three people sat in the seats.

How many seats were left?

_____

3. There were 37 acorns around the tree.

A squirrel hid 23 of them.

How many acorns were left?

_____

4. The mouse gathered 24 pieces of wheat and 32 pieces of grain.

How much did the mouse gather in all?

_____

5. Mark has 41 football cards, and Jerome has 53 football cards.

How many more cards does Jerome have than Mark?

_____

6. Lydia baked 48 cookies.

Her brothers ate 6 of them.

How many cookies does Lydia have left?

_____

Math Connection—Grade 2—RBP3780   www.summerbridgeactivities.com   ©RBP Books

2-Digit Addition and Subtraction Assessment

Solve the problems.

1.

$$\begin{array}{r} 31 \\ + 17 \\ \hline \end{array}\qquad \begin{array}{r} 54 \\ + 21 \\ \hline \end{array}\qquad \begin{array}{r} 72 \\ + 13 \\ \hline \end{array}\qquad \begin{array}{r} 23 \\ + 26 \\ \hline \end{array}\qquad \begin{array}{r} 44 \\ + 22 \\ \hline \end{array}$$

2.

$$\begin{array}{r} 65 \\ + 11 \\ \hline \end{array}\qquad \begin{array}{r} 21 \\ + 74 \\ \hline \end{array}\qquad \begin{array}{r} 39 \\ + 60 \\ \hline \end{array}\qquad \begin{array}{r} 31 \\ + 51 \\ \hline \end{array}\qquad \begin{array}{r} 33 \\ + 21 \\ \hline \end{array}$$

3.

$$\begin{array}{r} 29 \\ + 40 \\ \hline \end{array}\qquad \begin{array}{r} 32 \\ + 43 \\ \hline \end{array}\qquad \begin{array}{r} 63 \\ + 24 \\ \hline \end{array}\qquad \begin{array}{r} 16 \\ + 41 \\ \hline \end{array}\qquad \begin{array}{r} 37 \\ + 32 \\ \hline \end{array}$$

4.

$$\begin{array}{r} 55 \\ - 11 \\ \hline \end{array}\qquad \begin{array}{r} 46 \\ - 22 \\ \hline \end{array}\qquad \begin{array}{r} 86 \\ - 36 \\ \hline \end{array}\qquad \begin{array}{r} 79 \\ - 48 \\ \hline \end{array}\qquad \begin{array}{r} 88 \\ - 23 \\ \hline \end{array}$$

5.

$$\begin{array}{r} 57 \\ - 23 \\ \hline \end{array}\qquad \begin{array}{r} 62 \\ - 31 \\ \hline \end{array}\qquad \begin{array}{r} 96 \\ - 42 \\ \hline \end{array}\qquad \begin{array}{r} 79 \\ - 15 \\ \hline \end{array}\qquad \begin{array}{r} 34 \\ - 22 \\ \hline \end{array}$$

6.

$$\begin{array}{r} 68 \\ - 34 \\ \hline \end{array}\qquad \begin{array}{r} 57 \\ - 44 \\ \hline \end{array}\qquad \begin{array}{r} 38 \\ - 16 \\ \hline \end{array}\qquad \begin{array}{r} 97 \\ - 72 \\ \hline \end{array}\qquad \begin{array}{r} 66 \\ - 34 \\ \hline \end{array}$$

2-Digit Addition and Subtraction Assessment

Solve the problems.

1.

$$72 + 15$$ $$63 + 14$$ $$54 + 34$$ $$21 + 27$$ $$66 + 20$$

2.

$$25 + 42$$ $$44 + 34$$ $$38 + 40$$ $$26 + 51$$ $$40 + 27$$

3.

$$36 + 43$$ $$32 + 56$$ $$61 + 12$$ $$13 + 44$$ $$34 + 32$$

4.

$$39 - 14$$ $$55 - 21$$ $$88 - 25$$ $$99 - 18$$ $$86 - 23$$

5.

$$48 - 26$$ $$79 - 41$$ $$67 - 26$$ $$75 - 35$$ $$84 - 12$$

6.

$$78 - 26$$ $$57 - 42$$ $$39 - 12$$ $$94 - 62$$ $$66 - 25$$

2-Digit Addition with Regrouping

Solve the problems. Remember to regroup.

Add the ones.   If the total adds up to more than 9, regroup the number.   Add the tens.

tens 1

```
    2 8          2 8          1
  + 1 3        + 1 3          2 8
   11            1          + 1 3
                             4 1
```

1. 12 is _____ ten _____ ones

2. 16 is _____ ten _____ ones

3. 14 is _____ ten _____ ones

4. 10 is _____ ten _____ ones

5.
```
   35          44          52          73
 + 26        + 68        + 19        + 18
```

6.
```
   27          34          22          45
 + 56        + 49        + 59        + 38
```

2-Digit Addition with Regrouping

Solve the problems.

Remember to regroup the
sum of the ones.

You can do it!

1.	58 + 28	41 + 29	66 + 15	55 + 8	27 + 9

1.
58 + 28   41 + 29   66 + 15   55 + 8   27 + 9

2.
35 + 27   18 + 23   46 + 14   87 + 5   14 + 19

3.
68 + 28   47 + 47   65 + 28   16 + 17   56 + 29

4.
27 + 13   15 + 69   19 + 55   29 + 19   35 + 46

5.
56 + 25   39 + 25   14 + 9   87 + 33   63 + 18

Math Connection—Grade 2—RBP3780   www.summerbridgeactivities.com   ©RBP Books

2-Digit Addition with Regrouping
Solve the problems.

Remember to start with the ones.
Regroup. Then add the tens.

It's like adding apples and oranges!

1. $\begin{array}{r} 18 \\ +\ 17 \\ \hline \end{array}$	$\begin{array}{r} 11 \\ +\ 19 \\ \hline \end{array}$	$\begin{array}{r} 86 \\ +\ 47 \\ \hline \end{array}$	$\begin{array}{r} 38 \\ +\ 24 \\ \hline \end{array}$	$\begin{array}{r} 29 \\ +\ 63 \\ \hline \end{array}$
2. $\begin{array}{r} 13 \\ +\ 29 \\ \hline \end{array}$	$\begin{array}{r} 33 \\ +\ 59 \\ \hline \end{array}$	$\begin{array}{r} 58 \\ +\ 28 \\ \hline \end{array}$	$\begin{array}{r} 25 \\ +\ 25 \\ \hline \end{array}$	$\begin{array}{r} 28 \\ +\ 29 \\ \hline \end{array}$
3. $\begin{array}{r} 17 \\ +\ 33 \\ \hline \end{array}$	$\begin{array}{r} 74 \\ +\ 77 \\ \hline \end{array}$	$\begin{array}{r} 13 \\ +\ 9 \\ \hline \end{array}$	$\begin{array}{r} 7 \\ +\ 88 \\ \hline \end{array}$	$\begin{array}{r} 67 \\ +\ 69 \\ \hline \end{array}$
4. $\begin{array}{r} 44 \\ +\ 49 \\ \hline \end{array}$	$\begin{array}{r} 18 \\ +\ 19 \\ \hline \end{array}$	$\begin{array}{r} 48 \\ +\ 58 \\ \hline \end{array}$	$\begin{array}{r} 55 \\ +\ 66 \\ \hline \end{array}$	$\begin{array}{r} 99 \\ +\ 1 \\ \hline \end{array}$
5. $\begin{array}{r} 94 \\ +\ 17 \\ \hline \end{array}$	$\begin{array}{r} 77 \\ +\ 66 \\ \hline \end{array}$	$\begin{array}{r} 67 \\ +\ 67 \\ \hline \end{array}$	$\begin{array}{r} 92 \\ +\ 29 \\ \hline \end{array}$	$\begin{array}{r} 57 \\ +\ 47 \\ \hline \end{array}$

©RBP Books   www.summerbridgeactivities.com   Math Connection—Grade 2—RBP3780

2-Digit Addition with Some Regrouping

Solve the problems.

Remember to regroup if you need to.

We love this math stuff!

1.
$$16 + 10$$ $$19 + 42$$ $$64 + 92$$ $$24 + 18$$ $$62 + 71$$

2.
$$67 + 55$$ $$58 + 27$$ $$13 + 16$$ $$37 + 20$$ $$40 + 84$$

3.
$$40 + 28$$ $$67 + 53$$ $$29 + 39$$ $$19 + 18$$ $$32 + 48$$

4.
$$57 + 16$$ $$23 + 14$$ $$68 + 10$$ $$79 + 12$$ $$35 + 15$$

5.
$$82 + 14$$ $$97 + 17$$ $$46 + 12$$ $$35 + 20$$ $$51 + 47$$

6.
$$46 + 37$$ $$90 + 40$$ $$65 + 29$$ $$35 + 37$$ $$55 + 12$$

Number Puzzle

Complete the puzzle below.

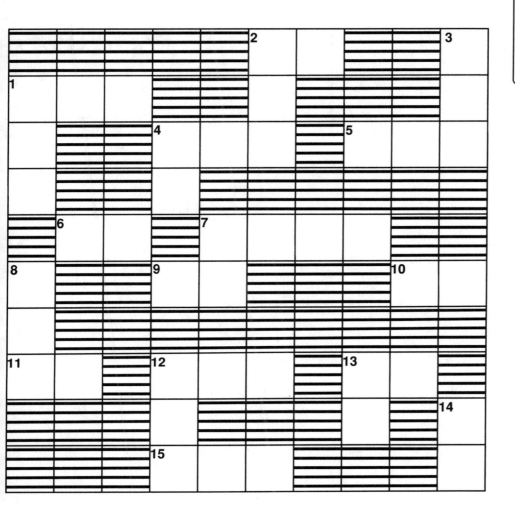

Wow! This looks like quite a puzzle!

Yeah, and here are the clues!

Across

1. $84 + 33 =$
2. $28 - 12 =$
4. $95 + 11 =$
5. $90 + 10 =$
6. $62 + 8 =$
7. $924 + 123 =$
9. $8 + 5 =$
10. $27 + 30 =$
11. $31 + 14 =$
12. $316 + 282 =$
13. $61 + 25 =$
15. $50 + 50 =$

Down

1. $67 + 48 =$
2. $79 + 47 =$
3. $94 + 26 =$
4. $32 - 20 =$
7. $84 - 71 =$
8. $167 + 117 =$
12. $210 + 321 =$
13. $93 - 7 =$
14. $29 - 16 =$

Addition with Regrouping

Solve the problems. Do your work in the box. Write your answer on the line.

  Read the problem carefully.
Then solve it.

I'm saving my money for a new basketball hoop!

1. Julie's mother planted 88 tulip bulbs and 19 roses.

How many total flowers did she plant?

_____

2. Mary paid 39¢ for buttons and 49¢ for ribbon.

How much did she spend?

_____

3. Kirk had two bags of peanuts.

One bag had 24 peanuts in it. The other had 69 in it.

How many peanuts did Kirk have?

_____

4. Amy had 49¢. She found 35¢.

How much money does she have?

_____

5. Mark found 19 worms yesterday and 14 this morning.

How many worms does Mark have?

_____

6. Cindy sold 47 tapes on Monday and 15 on Tuesday.

How many tapes did she sell?

_____

Math Connection—Grade 2—RBP3780   www.summerbridgeactivities.com   ©RBP Books

2-Digit Subtraction with Regrouping

Solve the problems. Remember to regroup.

Look at the ones. If you can not subtract the bottom from the top number, regroup.	To regroup, borrow 1 ten from the tens. Add it to the ones.	Subtract the ones first, then the tens.

You can't subtract 8 from 1.

$$\begin{array}{r} 6\ 1 \\ -2\ 8 \\ \hline \end{array}$$

1 ten from 6 tens leaves 5 tens. 1 ten plus 1 equals 11.

$$\begin{array}{r} {}^5\!6\ {}^1 1 \\ -2\ \ 8 \\ \hline \end{array}$$

11 take away 8 is 3. 5 tens minus 2 tens equals 3 tens.

$$\begin{array}{r} {}^5\!6\ {}^1 1 \\ -2\ \ 8 \\ \hline 3\ \ 3 \end{array}$$

1.
$$\begin{array}{r} {}^2\!\!3{}^1\!6 \\ -\ 17 \\ \hline \mathbf{19} \end{array}$$
$$\begin{array}{r} 33 \\ -\ 14 \\ \hline \end{array}$$
$$\begin{array}{r} 51 \\ -\ 34 \\ \hline \end{array}$$
$$\begin{array}{r} 53 \\ -\ 24 \\ \hline \end{array}$$
$$\begin{array}{r} 84 \\ -\ 27 \\ \hline \end{array}$$

2.
$$\begin{array}{r} 85 \\ -\ 26 \\ \hline \end{array}$$
$$\begin{array}{r} 64 \\ -\ 18 \\ \hline \end{array}$$
$$\begin{array}{r} 67 \\ -\ 29 \\ \hline \end{array}$$
$$\begin{array}{r} 30 \\ -\ 18 \\ \hline \end{array}$$
$$\begin{array}{r} 34 \\ -\ 17 \\ \hline \end{array}$$

3.
$$\begin{array}{r} 61 \\ -\ 32 \\ \hline \end{array}$$
$$\begin{array}{r} 43 \\ -\ 34 \\ \hline \end{array}$$
$$\begin{array}{r} 20 \\ -\ 12 \\ \hline \end{array}$$
$$\begin{array}{r} 35 \\ -\ 16 \\ \hline \end{array}$$
$$\begin{array}{r} 43 \\ -\ 28 \\ \hline \end{array}$$

4.
$$\begin{array}{r} 83 \\ -\ 55 \\ \hline \end{array}$$
$$\begin{array}{r} 52 \\ -\ 35 \\ \hline \end{array}$$
$$\begin{array}{r} 63 \\ -\ 26 \\ \hline \end{array}$$
$$\begin{array}{r} 77 \\ -\ 38 \\ \hline \end{array}$$
$$\begin{array}{r} 66 \\ -\ 48 \\ \hline \end{array}$$

2-Digit Subtraction with Regrouping

Solve the problems.

 Look at the ones. If you can't subtract, regroup. 96 is regrouped as 8 tens and 16 ones. Now you can subtract.

 Hurray for regrouping!

1.
$$\begin{array}{r} \overset{8}{\cancel{9}}\overset{1}{6} \\ -\ 28 \\ \hline \mathbf{68} \end{array}$$
$$\begin{array}{r} 84 \\ -\ 39 \\ \hline \end{array}$$
$$\begin{array}{r} 47 \\ -\ 18 \\ \hline \end{array}$$
$$\begin{array}{r} 64 \\ -\ 47 \\ \hline \end{array}$$
$$\begin{array}{r} 22 \\ -\ 8 \\ \hline \end{array}$$

2.
$$\begin{array}{r} 95 \\ -\ 47 \\ \hline \end{array}$$
$$\begin{array}{r} 34 \\ -\ 19 \\ \hline \end{array}$$
$$\begin{array}{r} 74 \\ -\ 18 \\ \hline \end{array}$$
$$\begin{array}{r} 43 \\ -\ 15 \\ \hline \end{array}$$
$$\begin{array}{r} 31 \\ -\ 17 \\ \hline \end{array}$$

3.
$$\begin{array}{r} 62 \\ -\ 36 \\ \hline \end{array}$$
$$\begin{array}{r} 85 \\ -\ 46 \\ \hline \end{array}$$
$$\begin{array}{r} 74 \\ -\ 28 \\ \hline \end{array}$$
$$\begin{array}{r} 72 \\ -\ 8 \\ \hline \end{array}$$
$$\begin{array}{r} 80 \\ -\ 18 \\ \hline \end{array}$$

4.
$$\begin{array}{r} 61 \\ -\ 33 \\ \hline \end{array}$$
$$\begin{array}{r} 50 \\ -13 \\ \hline \end{array}$$
$$\begin{array}{r} 62 \\ -\ 3 \\ \hline \end{array}$$
$$\begin{array}{r} 72 \\ -\ 14 \\ \hline \end{array}$$
$$\begin{array}{r} 31 \\ -\ 18 \\ \hline \end{array}$$

5.
$$\begin{array}{r} 47 \\ -\ 29 \\ \hline \end{array}$$
$$\begin{array}{r} 63 \\ -\ 37 \\ \hline \end{array}$$
$$\begin{array}{r} 71 \\ -\ 35 \\ \hline \end{array}$$
$$\begin{array}{r} 90 \\ -\ 55 \\ \hline \end{array}$$
$$\begin{array}{r} 61 \\ -\ 19 \\ \hline \end{array}$$

Math Connection—Grade 2—RBP3780 www.summerbridgeactivities.com ©RBP Books

2-Digit Subtraction with Some Regrouping

Solve the problems.

Remember to regroup
if you need to.

1.
$$\begin{array}{r} 25 \\ -13 \\ \hline \end{array}$$
$$\begin{array}{r} 30 \\ -19 \\ \hline \end{array}$$
$$\begin{array}{r} 56 \\ -42 \\ \hline \end{array}$$
$$\begin{array}{r} 83 \\ -38 \\ \hline \end{array}$$
$$\begin{array}{r} 77 \\ -44 \\ \hline \end{array}$$

2.
$$\begin{array}{r} 46 \\ -18 \\ \hline \end{array}$$
$$\begin{array}{r} 63 \\ -38 \\ \hline \end{array}$$
$$\begin{array}{r} 88 \\ -38 \\ \hline \end{array}$$
$$\begin{array}{r} 64 \\ -25 \\ \hline \end{array}$$
$$\begin{array}{r} 53 \\ -26 \\ \hline \end{array}$$

3.
$$\begin{array}{r} 44 \\ -26 \\ \hline \end{array}$$
$$\begin{array}{r} 75 \\ -67 \\ \hline \end{array}$$
$$\begin{array}{r} 23 \\ -13 \\ \hline \end{array}$$
$$\begin{array}{r} 67 \\ -39 \\ \hline \end{array}$$
$$\begin{array}{r} 84 \\ -15 \\ \hline \end{array}$$

4.
$$\begin{array}{r} 66 \\ -28 \\ \hline \end{array}$$
$$\begin{array}{r} 32 \\ -13 \\ \hline \end{array}$$
$$\begin{array}{r} 76 \\ -29 \\ \hline \end{array}$$
$$\begin{array}{r} 57 \\ -45 \\ \hline \end{array}$$
$$\begin{array}{r} 61 \\ -28 \\ \hline \end{array}$$

5.
$$\begin{array}{r} 95 \\ -27 \\ \hline \end{array}$$
$$\begin{array}{r} 67 \\ -27 \\ \hline \end{array}$$
$$\begin{array}{r} 47 \\ -19 \\ \hline \end{array}$$
$$\begin{array}{r} 51 \\ -33 \\ \hline \end{array}$$
$$\begin{array}{r} 93 \\ -46 \\ \hline \end{array}$$

Subtraction Practice with Some Regrouping

Solve the problems.

Think! Regroup if you need to.

1.
24	39	47	50	22
− 12	− 27	− 44	− 38	− 11

2.
67	43	55	72	33
− 39	− 26	− 38	− 14	− 16

3.
42	94	32	87	42
− 16	− 68	− 14	− 61	− 16

4.
44	60	54	65	96
− 19	− 31	− 26	− 26	− 18

5.
84	68	98	72	81
− 32	− 39	− 46	− 18	− 16

Math Connection—Grade 2—RBP3780   www.summerbridgeactivities.com   ©RBP Books

Name			Date	

Subtraction Practice

Solve the problems.

 More subtraction practice!
Remember to regroup if you
need to.

1.	72 − 9	47 − 28	61 − 42	58 − 39	33 − 14
2.	54 − 19	51 − 38	62 − 30	43 − 26	42 − 29
3.	75 − 33	71 − 23	72 − 56	38 − 24	87 − 45
4.	35 − 16	88 − 59	51 − 18	62 − 35	45 − 27
5.	94 − 18	49 − 24	38 − 13	82 − 47	67 − 42
6.	82 − 23	40 − 12	95 − 36	64 − 23	70 − 13

Subtraction with Regrouping

Solve the problems. Do your work in the box. Write your answer on the line.

In the forest there are 92 deer. Twenty-five of them ran out of the forest. How many deer are still in the forest?

$$\begin{array}{r} \overset{8}{\cancel{9}}{}^{1}2 \\ -\ 25 \\ \hline \mathbf{67} \end{array}$$

Read the problem. Set it up like any other subtraction problem. Regroup if you need to.

1. Eighty-four peaches were on our tree.

We picked 68.

How many peaches were left on the tree?

_____

2. Megan collected 78 bottle caps. Alex collected 29.

How many more did Megan collect than Alex?

_____

3. Eighty-six children went swimming.

Nineteen of them went home.

How many children were still in the pool?

_____

4. Forty-two cans of fruit were on the shelf.

A lady bought 14 of them.

How many cans were left on the shelf?

_____

5. My box of animal crackers had 41 crackers.

Justin's box had 67.

How many more animal crackers did Justin have?

_____

6. I lined up 52 dominos.

Fourteen of them fell.

How many dominos did not fall?

_____

Math Connection—Grade 2—RBP3780   www.summerbridgeactivities.com   ©RBP Books

2-Digit Addition and Subtraction Practice

Solve the problems.

Remember to start with the
ones and regroup if necessary.

I'm sure you'll have
no problem finishing
these problems!

1.	47 + 34	59 + 36	72 + 28	64 + 29	25 + 37
2.	56 + 58	27 + 63	33 + 69	28 + 87	78 + 19
3.	84 + 26	97 + 16	54 + 27	73 + 39	95 + 15
4.	82 − 17	71 − 26	60 − 39	93 − 47	84 − 36
5.	73 − 35	52 − 18	91 − 38	88 − 29	74 − 31
6.	65 − 27	72 − 45	81 − 63	70 − 54	97 − 58

2-Digit Addition and Subtraction Practice

Solve the problems.

 Watch the signs. Look at the answer and ask yourself if it makes sense.

 I bet you can do these problems in a snap!

1.
56	48	63	88	27
+ 37	+ 35	+ 58	+ 39	+ 57

2.
59	36	45	46	75
+ 28	+ 67	+ 47	+ 85	+ 13

3.
82	97	29	73	96
+ 23	+ 37	+ 36	+ 49	+ 25

4.
70	81	67	54	82
− 18	− 22	− 33	− 17	− 56

5.
71	52	91	78	74
− 38	− 26	− 35	− 49	− 26

6.
65	92	83	60	57
− 23	− 45	− 65	− 14	− 38

Math Connection—Grade 2—RBP3780   www.summerbridgeactivities.com

Name _____ Date _____

2-Digit Addition and Subtraction Problem Solving

Solve the problems. Do your work in the box. Write your answer on the line.

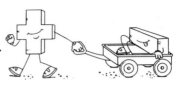

 Drawing a picture or picturing the problem in your head may help you decide whether you need to add or subtract.

1. The class did 36 math problems on Monday and 45 problems on Wednesday.

How many math problems did they complete?

_____

2. Kelsey completed 36 math problems.

He missed 7 of the problems.

How many problems were correct?

_____

3. Jillian completed 81 math problems, plus 37 additional problems.

How many problems did she complete?

_____

4. There are 27 students in the class.

Nineteen students got all the problems correct.

How many students missed at least one problem?

_____

5. Mrs. Tripp had 96 math papers to grade.

She graded 39 papers on Tuesday.

How many more papers did she have left to grade?

_____

6. Each student is trying to complete 1,000 math problems in one month.

Nick completed 25 the first day, 34 the second day, and 27 the third day.

How many problems has Nick completed so far?

_____

www.summerbridgeactivities.com   Math Connection—Grade 2—RBP3780

2-Digit Addition and Subtraction Assessment
Solve the problems.

1.

$$58 + 37$$ $$47 + 49$$ $$57 + 18$$ $$66 + 35$$ $$25 + 37$$

2.

$$56 + 46$$ $$33 + 67$$ $$48 + 39$$ $$29 + 59$$ $$76 + 19$$

3.

$$85 + 36$$ $$94 + 26$$ $$54 + 27$$ $$73 + 39$$ $$95 + 15$$

4.

$$73 - 27$$ $$51 - 16$$ $$50 - 29$$ $$82 - 37$$ $$74 - 34$$

5.

$$63 - 35$$ $$92 - 68$$ $$61 - 34$$ $$88 - 39$$ $$52 - 21$$

6.

$$53 - 36$$ $$62 - 26$$ $$81 - 49$$ $$70 - 22$$ $$95 - 56$$

Math Connection—Grade 2—RBP3780   www.summerbridgeactivities.com   ©RBP Books

2-Digit Addition and Subtraction Problem Solving

Solve the problems.

We love this math stuff!

1.	49 + 28	55 + 39	27 + 46	67 + 37	48 + 22
2.	65 + 56	47 + 67	39 + 36	48 + 59	79 + 19
3.	58 + 37	97 + 16	55 + 47	72 + 49	96 + 28
4.	84 − 37	61 − 35	72 − 29	80 − 23	56 − 38
5.	64 − 25	91 − 46	73 − 24	77 − 49	42 − 26
6.	70 − 34	52 − 24	87 − 39	74 − 27	65 − 36

RBP Books   www.summerbridgeactivities.com   Math Connection—Grade 2—RBP3780

Reading a Bar Graph

Look at the graph. Answer the questions.

 A graph is a good way to organize information. Each shaded square in this graph equals one book.

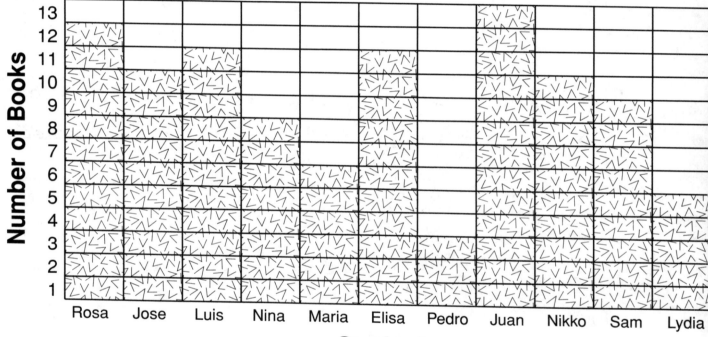

Books We've Read

1. How many books did Elisa read? _____

2. Who read more books, Luis or Nina? _____

3. Who read the most books? _____

4. Who read the fewest books? _____

5. How many books did Rosa, Juan, and Maria read altogether? _____

Math Connection—Grade 2—RBP3780   www.summerbridgeactivities.com   ©RBP Books

Reading a Calendar
Read the calendar. Answer the questions.

July

Sunday	Monday	Tuesday	Wednesday	Thursday	Friday	Saturday
				1	2	3
4	5	6	7	8	9	10
11	12	13	14	15	16	17
18	19	20	21	22	23	24
25	26	27	28	29	30	31

1. What month does this calendar show? _____

2. On what day of the week does the month start? _____

3. On what day of the week is July 4th? _____

4. How many days are in July? _____

5. How many Saturdays are in July? _____

6. If today is July 14th, how many days are left in the month? _____

Recognizing Shapes

Count the shapes. Write the number.

1. How many squares? _____

2. How many circles? _____

3. How many rectangles? _____

4. How many triangles? _____

IT'S ALIVE!!

- Color the circles yellow.
- Color the triangles blue.
- Color the squares red.
- Color the rectangles green.

Math Connection—Grade 2—RBP3780   www.summerbridgeactivities.com   ©RBP Books

Exploring Geometric Solids

Circle the shape that is on the bottom.

 Think about what shape is on the bottom.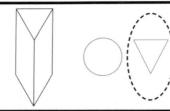

1.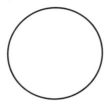

2.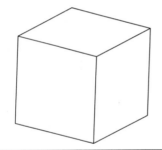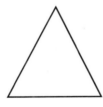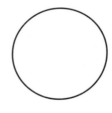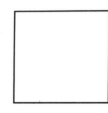

3.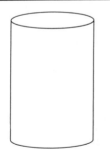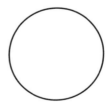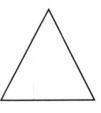

4.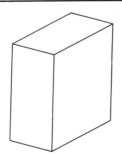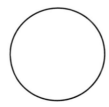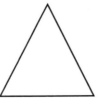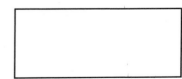

Exploring Volume

Circle the one that holds the most.

 We measure liquid by <u>volume</u>.

 Math helped me mix up this delicious cake! It can help you too!

1.

2.

3.

4.

Math Connection—Grade 2—RBP3780   www.summerbridgeactivities.com   ©RBP Books

Measuring with Inches

Measure around each shape. Then add.

Try to measure some things around your room!

1.

_____ inches

```
inches  1    2    3    4    5    6
```

2.

```
inches  1    2
```

_____ inches

3.

```
inches  1    2    3
```

_____ inches

4.

```
...ches  1    2    3    4    5
```

_____ inches

www.summerbridgeactivities.com   Math Connection—Grade 2—RBP3780

Measuring with Inches

Measure around each shape. Then add.

 Be sure to put the ruler at
the beginning of the line.

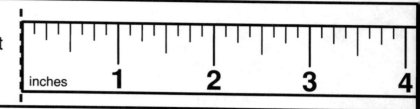

1.

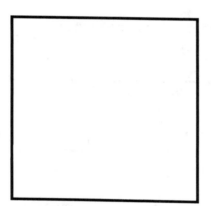

__2__ + _____ + _____ + _____ = _____

2.

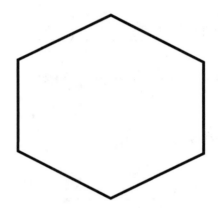

___ + ___ + ___ + ___ + ___ + ___ = ____

3.

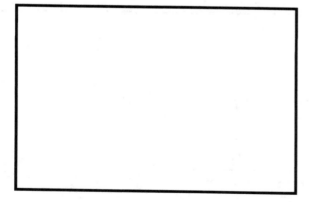

_____ + ____ + ____ + ____ = ____

4.

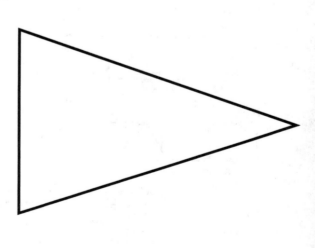

_____ + ____ + ____ = ____

Math Connection—Grade 2—RBP3780   www.summerbridgeactivities.com   ©RBP Books

Measuring with Centimeters

 Be sure to line up the centimeter ruler like you do the inch ruler.

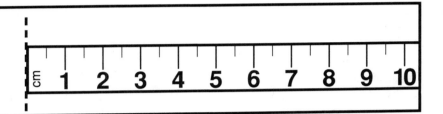

Measure these lines with a centimeter ruler.

Write each line length on the blank.

1. _____ = _____ cm

2. _____ = _____ cm

3. _____ = _____ cm

4. _____ = _____ cm

5. _____ = _____ cm

Measure the shapes with a centimeter ruler. Then add.

7.  ____ + ____ + ____ = ____ cm

6.

8.

 ___ + ___ + ___ + ___ = ____ cm

___ + ___ + ___ + ___ = ____ cm

Problem Solving with Measurement

Use your ruler to draw the pictures.

1.

Draw a square with each side
measuring 1 inch.

2.

Draw a picture of a fence that is
3 inches long.

3.

Draw a tree that is 2 inches high.

4.

Draw a diagonal line that is 4
inches long.

Name _____   Date _____

3-Digit Addition
Solve each problem.

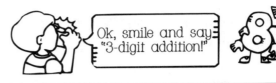

Ok, smile and say "3-digit addition!"

1. Add the ones.   **2.** Add the tens.   **3.** Add the hundreds.

```
    8 3 |5|          8 |3| 5          |8| 3 5
  + 1 4 |2|        + 1 |4| 2        + |1| 4 2
        |7|            |7| 7          |9| 7 7
```

1.
```
   614        730        212        723        500
 + 112      + 233      + 764      + 102      + 427
```

2.
```
   200        541        132        404        237
 + 300      + 136      +  21      + 171      + 131
```

3.
```
   942        851        584        422        247
 +  31      + 148      + 113      + 244      + 111
```

4.
```
   867        166        137        542        700
 + 102      +  12      + 621      + 321      + 200
```

5.
```
   226        524        446        604        231
 + 571      + 264      + 351      + 172      +  21
```

www.summerbridgeactivities.com   Math Connection—Grade 2—RBP3780

3-Digit Addition with Some Regrouping

Solve each problem.

1. Add the ones. Regroup if you need to.	2. Add the tens. Regroup if you need to.	3. Add the hundreds.
6 ¹4 | 5 + 2 8 | 7 **2**	¹6 | ¹4 | 5 + 2 | 8 | 7 **3 2**	¹6 | 4 5 + 2 | 8 7 **9** | **3 2**

1.

245	552	368	163	472
+ 83	+ 212	+ 107	+ 16	+ 309

2.

210	221	828	363	168
+ 116	+ 182	+ 135	+ 236	+ 109

3.

659	234	259	182	849
+ 139	+ 524	+ 12	+ 145	+ 90

4.

236	547	473	783	153
+ 126	+ 238	+ 364	+ 113	+ 354

5.

254	205	254	448	613
+ 106	+ 677	+ 159	+ 121	+ 29

3-Digit Addition Problem Solving

Solve the problems. Do your work in the box. Write your answer on the line.

 Read the problem carefully.
Then add.
Regroup if you need to.

I ♥ Word Problems!

---

1. There are 346 students in the lower grades and 416 students in the upper grades.

How many students are there in all?

_____

2. 236 students had a field trip on Tuesday. 127 students had a field trip on Friday.

How many students had a field trip this week?

_____

---

3. 119 students are in the band.

57 students are in the chorus.

How many students are in the music program altogether?

_____

4. 318 students ride the first bus.

229 students ride the second bus.

How many students ride the bus in all?

_____

---

5. 112 children are in the morning kindergarten classes.

124 are in the afternoon kindergarten classes.

How many kindergartners are there in all?

_____

6. The second graders checked out 212 books from the library.

The third graders checked out 178 books.

How many books did the students in grades 2 and 3 check out in all?

_____

3-Digit Subtraction

Solve each problem.

1. Subtract the ones.   **2.** Subtract the tens.   **3.** Subtract the hundreds.

```
  6 7 | 0 |          6 | 7 | 0          | 6 | 7   0
- 2 4 | 0 |        - 2 | 4 | 0        - | 2 | 4   0
      |   |            |   |            |   |
      | 0 |            | 3 | 0          | 4 | 3   0
```

1.
864	286	648	984	748
− 123	− 133	− 141	− 400	− 124

2.
576	698	379	840	695
− 201	− 568	− 141	− 130	− 645

3.
127	762	844	539	775
− 13	− 241	− 523	− 425	− 225

4.
572	937	623	254	742
− 122	− 725	− 102	− 12	− 112

5.
245	667	263	314	867
− 124	− 324	− 152	− 13	− 120

3-Digit Subtraction with Regrouping
Solve each problem.

1. Subtract the ones. Regroup if you need to.   **2.** Subtract the tens. Regroup if you need to.   **3.** Subtract the hundreds.

I can take 7 away from 9. I don't need to regroup.

$$\begin{array}{r} 5\ 1\ \boxed{9} \\ -\ 2\ 8\ \boxed{7} \\ \hline \boxed{2} \end{array}$$

I can't take 8 tens from 1 ten, so I borrow 1 hundred from 5 hundreds. Then I regroup to make 11 tens.

$$\begin{array}{r} ^4\cancel{5}\ ^1\boxed{1}\ 9 \\ -\ 2\ \boxed{8}\ 7 \\ \hline \boxed{3}\ 2 \end{array}$$

$$\begin{array}{r} ^4\boxed{\cancel{5}}\ ^11\ 9 \\ -\ \boxed{2}\ 8\ 7 \\ \hline \boxed{2}\ 3\ 2 \end{array}$$

1.

$$\begin{array}{r} 528 \\ -\ 134 \\ \hline \end{array}$$
$$\begin{array}{r} 437 \\ -\ 129 \\ \hline \end{array}$$
$$\begin{array}{r} 644 \\ -\ 246 \\ \hline \end{array}$$
$$\begin{array}{r} 434 \\ -\ 225 \\ \hline \end{array}$$
$$\begin{array}{r} 942 \\ -\ 367 \\ \hline \end{array}$$

2.

$$\begin{array}{r} 410 \\ -\ 132 \\ \hline \end{array}$$
$$\begin{array}{r} 840 \\ -\ 38 \\ \hline \end{array}$$
$$\begin{array}{r} 864 \\ -\ 239 \\ \hline \end{array}$$
$$\begin{array}{r} 717 \\ -\ 226 \\ \hline \end{array}$$
$$\begin{array}{r} 547 \\ -\ 139 \\ \hline \end{array}$$

3.

$$\begin{array}{r} 875 \\ -\ 406 \\ \hline \end{array}$$
$$\begin{array}{r} 141 \\ -\ 57 \\ \hline \end{array}$$
$$\begin{array}{r} 843 \\ -\ 327 \\ \hline \end{array}$$
$$\begin{array}{r} 648 \\ -\ 252 \\ \hline \end{array}$$
$$\begin{array}{r} 286 \\ -\ 137 \\ \hline \end{array}$$

4.

$$\begin{array}{r} 984 \\ -\ 296 \\ \hline \end{array}$$
$$\begin{array}{r} 885 \\ -\ 147 \\ \hline \end{array}$$
$$\begin{array}{r} 671 \\ -\ 366 \\ \hline \end{array}$$
$$\begin{array}{r} 352 \\ -\ 204 \\ \hline \end{array}$$
$$\begin{array}{r} 622 \\ -\ 144 \\ \hline \end{array}$$

5.

$$\begin{array}{r} 142 \\ -\ 36 \\ \hline \end{array}$$
$$\begin{array}{r} 328 \\ -\ 182 \\ \hline \end{array}$$
$$\begin{array}{r} 555 \\ -\ 388 \\ \hline \end{array}$$
$$\begin{array}{r} 210 \\ -\ 97 \\ \hline \end{array}$$
$$\begin{array}{r} 332 \\ -\ 146 \\ \hline \end{array}$$

3-Digit Subtraction Problem Solving

Solve the problems. Do your work in the box. Write your answer on the line.

Read the problem carefully.
Then subtract.
Regroup if you need to.

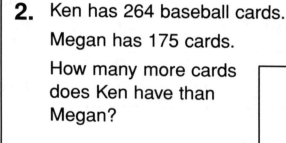 Ok, smile and say "3-digit subtraction!"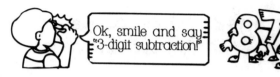

---

1. Ryan had 427 baseball cards.

He sold 109 cards.

How many cards does he have left?

_____

2. Ken has 264 baseball cards.

Megan has 175 cards.

How many more cards does Ken have than Megan?

_____

---

3. Tran had 822 pennies.

He took 800 pennies to the bank.

How many pennies does he have left?

_____

4. Seth has 731 bottle caps.

Brad has 947 bottle caps.

How many more bottle caps does Brad have than Seth?

_____

---

5. Kate has saved 421 dollars.

Her older sister has saved 540 dollars.

How many dollars less does Kate have than her sister?

_____

6. Justin got $127 for his birthday.

He spent $82 dollars on a new bike.

How much does he have left?

_____

3-Digit Addition and Subtraction Practice

Solve each problem.

Watch the signs!
Regroup if you need to.

We love this math stuff!

1.	122 + 312	325 − 132	745 − 146	525 + 414	109 − 98
2.	229 + 149	670 − 384	639 + 327	129 − 30	598 + 319
3.	243 + 138	111 − 62	775 − 187	622 + 219	330 − 129
4.	958 − 169	148 + 58	394 − 139	227 + 272	136 + 134
5.	296 − 98	413 + 146	480 − 246	147 + 64	336 + 136

3-Digit Addition and Subtraction Practice

Solve the problems.

Remember to start with the ones,
then the tens, then the hundreds.
Regroup if you need to.

I bet you can do
these problems
in a snap!

1.
```
  233        429        782        324        883
+ 476      + 128      + 137      + 473      + 149
```

2.
```
  842        711        620        423        907
− 279      − 362      − 287      − 185      − 468
```

3.
```
  271        779        564        178        981
+ 188      + 172      + 147      + 446      + 176
```

4.
```
  834        703        513        800        614
− 287      − 349      − 227      − 179      − 275
```

5.
```
  743        238        732        909        612
+ 827      + 137      − 567      − 219      + 374
```

3-Digit Addition and Subtraction Practice

Solve the problems.

 Knowing your basic math facts makes these problems a snap!

1.
$$558 + 124$$ $$387 + 293$$ $$346 + 229$$ $$340 + 379$$ $$847 + 239$$

2.
$$801 - 284$$ $$740 - 227$$ $$623 - 178$$ $$731 - 182$$ $$552 - 174$$

3.
$$235 + 447$$ $$226 + 423$$ $$125 + 919$$ $$105 + 810$$ $$116 + 904$$

4.
$$912 - 608$$ $$218 - 129$$ $$410 - 117$$ $$843 - 276$$ $$560 - 388$$

5.
$$700 - 197$$ $$326 + 259$$ $$463 + 531$$ $$833 - 246$$ $$734 - 165$$

3-Digit Addition and Subtraction Problem Solving

Solve the problems. Do your work in the box. Write your answer on the line.

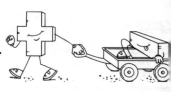

1. Jill picked 324 apples. Ted picked 271 apples.

How many apples did they pick in all?

_____ apples in all

```
  3 2 4
+ 2 7 1
  5 9 5
```

2. On the first day of our trip we drove 241 miles.

On the second day we drove 452 miles.

How many more miles did we drive the second day?

_____ miles

3. We counted 332 cows in one field.

In another field we counted 164 cows.

How many cows did we count in all?

_____ cows

4. Mrs. Hill had 567 candles for sale in her store.

By the end of the day she had 325.

How many candles did she sell?

_____ candles

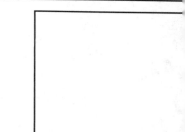

5. There were 724 people at the ball game.

When it began to rain 510 people left.

How many people stayed at the game?

_____ people

3-Digit Addition and Subtraction Assessment

Solve the problems.

1.   443   513   125   260   431
       + 123   + 371   + 342   + 238   + 168

2.   537   698   729   776   839
       + 184   + 231   + 193   + 248   + 486

3.   887   895   973   798   985
       − 124   − 220   − 362   − 455   − 531

4.   602   832   882   733   510
       − 188   − 167   − 294   − 196   − 218

Solve the problem. Do your work in the box. Write your answer on the line.

5. We drove 334 miles on the first day of our trip.

On the second day we drove 249 miles.

How many miles did we drive altogether?

_____

6. Josie had 802 pennies.

Jimmy had 789 pennies.

How many more pennies did Josie have?

_____

RBP Books   www.summerbridgeactivities.com   Math Connection—Grade 2—RBP3780

3-Digit Addition and Subtraction Assessment
Solve the problems.

1. 303   432   135   450   237
       + 263 + 231 + 312 + 218 + 160

2. 638   578   786   673   892
       + 285 + 247 + 296 + 168 + 179

3. 894   876   674   598   973
       − 223 − 261 − 302 − 352 − 231

4. 617   731   802   714   500
       − 289 − 185 − 262 − 176 − 382

Solve the problem. Do your work in the box. Write your answer on the line.

5. Sam has 368 baseball cards.
Josh has 299 baseball cards.
How many more cards does Sam have than Josh?

_____

6. Derek collected 298 cans.
Kaylee collected 479 cans.
How many cans did they collect together?

_____

Math Connection—Grade 2—RBP3780   www.summerbridgeactivities.com   © RBP Books

Name ____________________ Date ____________________

Exploring Fractions

Write the correct fraction.

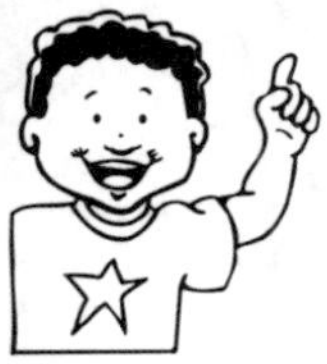

A fraction tells parts of a whole.
The top number tells how many parts are shaded.
The bottom number tells how many parts in all.

Parts shaded ⟶ **1**

Parts in all ⟶ **4**

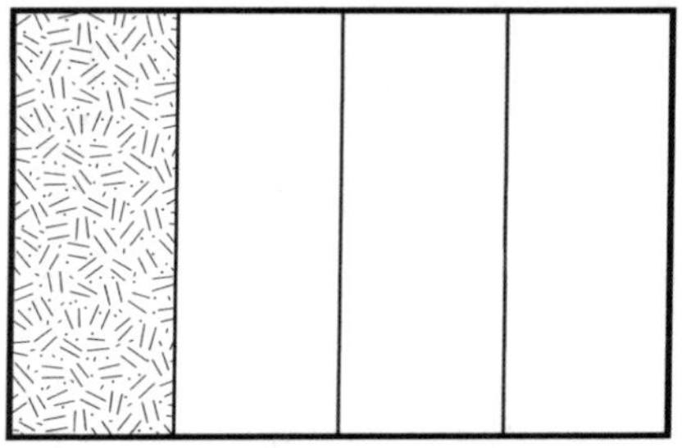

1. 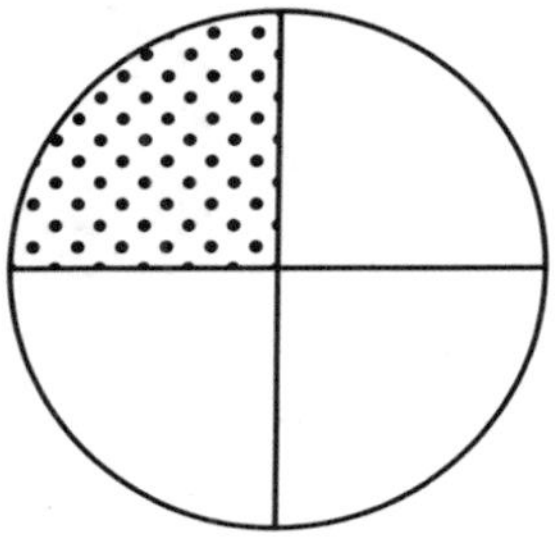 $\frac{__}{4}$

2. 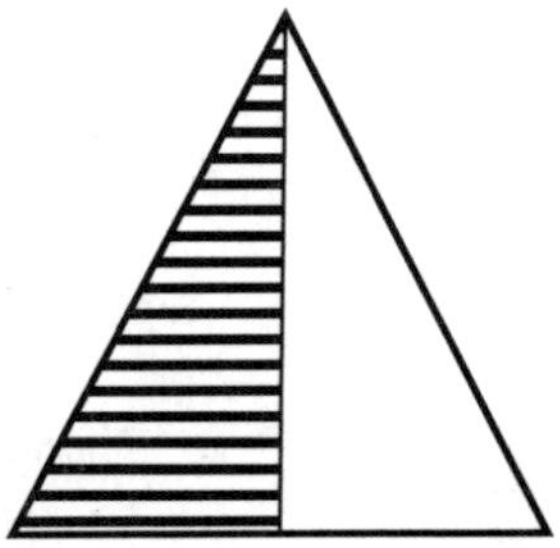 $\frac{__}{2}$

3. 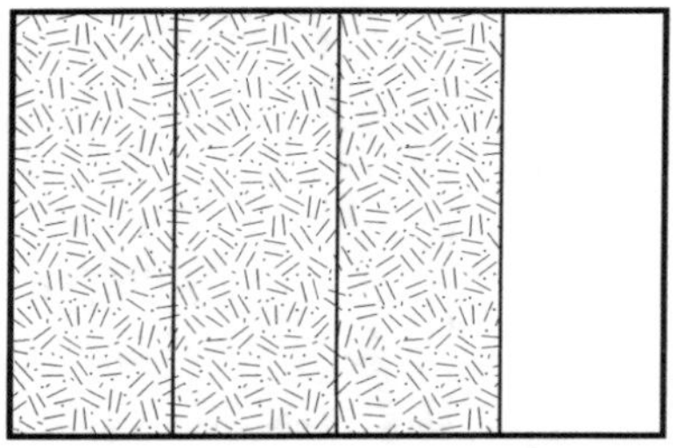 $\frac{__}{4}$

4. 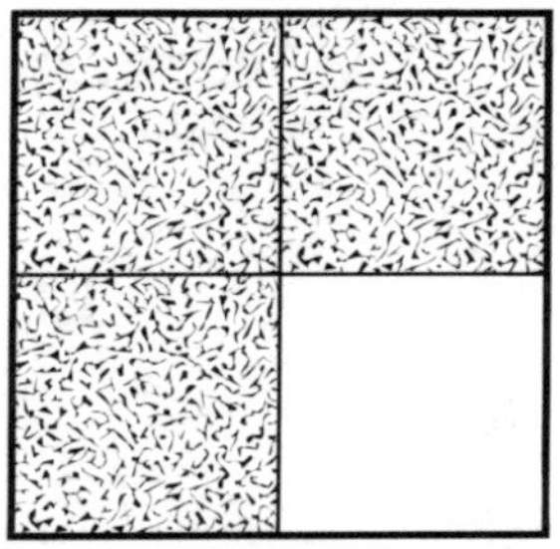 $\frac{__}{4}$

5. 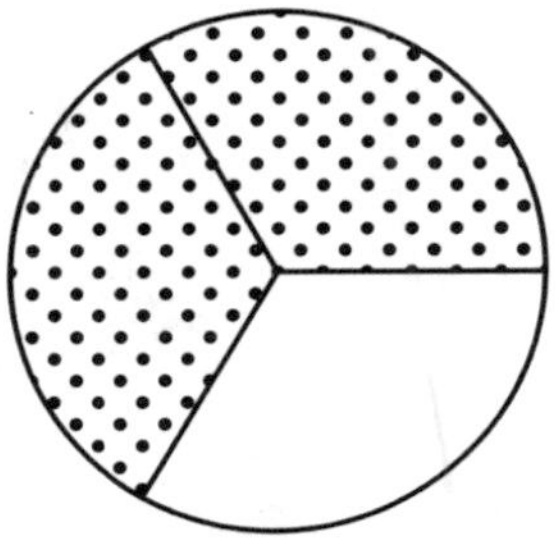 $\frac{__}{3}$

6. 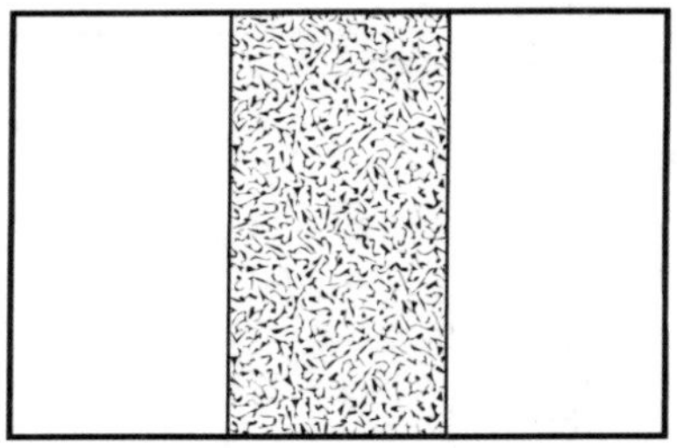 $\frac{__}{3}$

Exploring Fractions

Circle the fraction that tells how much is shaded.

There are four parts, so the bottom number is 4.

One part is shaded.

The answer is $\frac{1}{4}$.

$\dfrac{1}{2}$ $\dfrac{1}{3}$ $\dfrac{1}{4}$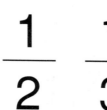

1.
$\dfrac{1}{2}$ $\dfrac{1}{4}$ $\dfrac{1}{3}$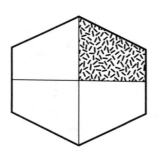

2.
$\dfrac{1}{3}$ $\dfrac{2}{3}$ $\dfrac{1}{2}$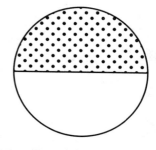

3.
$\dfrac{2}{4}$ $\dfrac{3}{4}$ $\dfrac{1}{4}$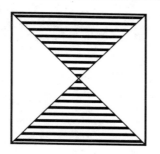

4.
$\dfrac{1}{4}$ $\dfrac{2}{4}$ $\dfrac{3}{4}$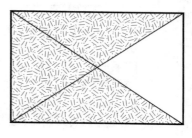

5.
$\dfrac{1}{3}$ $\dfrac{1}{2}$ $\dfrac{2}{3}$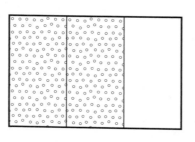

6.
$\dfrac{1}{3}$ $\dfrac{2}{3}$ $\dfrac{1}{2}$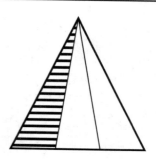

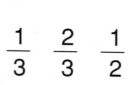

Exploring Fractions

Circle the correct fraction.

I love fractions this much!

Look at how many parts make up the whole. That is the bottom number. Then think about how many parts are being talked about. That is the top number.

1.

How much of the sandwich is left?

$\frac{1}{2}$ $\frac{1}{3}$ $\frac{1}{4}$

2.

How much water is in the cup?

$\frac{1}{2}$ $\frac{1}{4}$ $\frac{3}{4}$

3.

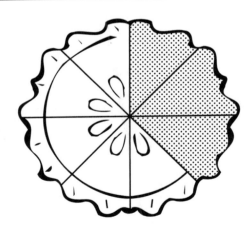

How much pie is left?

$\frac{1}{2}$ $\frac{5}{8}$ $\frac{1}{4}$

4.

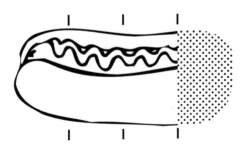

How much of the hot dog has been eaten?

$\frac{1}{2}$ $\frac{1}{3}$ $\frac{1}{4}$

Name _____ Date _____

Exploring Fractions
Color the shape to show the fraction.

 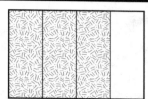

 I colored 3 parts because the fraction shows three-fourths.

$$\frac{3}{4}$$

1.

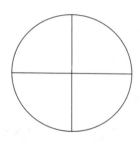

$$\frac{3}{4}$$

2.

$$\frac{1}{3}$$

3.

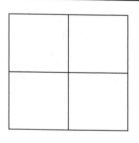

$$\frac{1}{4}$$

4.

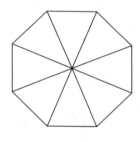

$$\frac{5}{8}$$

5.

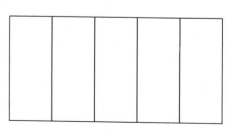

$$\frac{2}{5}$$

6.

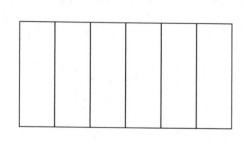

$$\frac{1}{6}$$

www.summerbridgeactivities.com ©RBP Books

Exploring Probability

Look at the spinner. Answer the questions.

To have the same chance
of spinning each color, the
spaces all need to be equal.

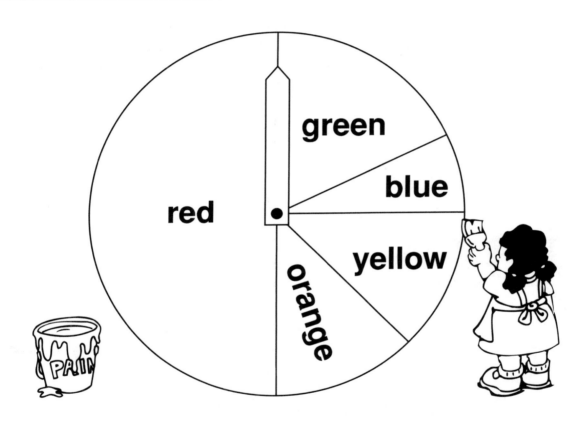

1. Which color will probably come up most often?_____

2. Which color will probably come up least often?_____

3. Which two colors will probably come up the same number of times?_____

4. Do you think you would land on green or yellow more often?_____

Exploring Probability

Flip a coin 10 times. Record the results.

 Because there are 2 possible results from flipping a coin, and heads is one of the possibilities, we say: "There is 1 out of 2 chances to get heads."

Heads	Tails

1. How many times did heads come up? _____

2. How many times did tails come up? _____

3. What do you think would happen if you flipped the coin 10 more times?

   _____

4. Flip the coin 10 more times. Record the results. Write what happened.

   _____

Math Connection—Grade 2—RBP3780 www.summerbridgeactivities.com ©RBP Books

Name _____   Date _____

Recognizing Patterns
Find the pattern.

 What will the ninth shape be? Sometimes I draw the pattern out.
Sometimes I just think in my head.
The ninth shape will be a ❑ (square).

1. What will the eighth shape be? ____

2. What will the tenth shape be? _____

3. What will the next shape be? _____

4. What will the seventh shape be? ____

5. What will the ninth shape be? _____

6. What will the tenth shape be? _____

RBP Books   www.summerbridgeactivities.com   Math Connection—Grade 2—RBP3780

Number Patterns

Find the number pattern.

The next numbers are 12, 15, and 18.
The pattern is <u>plus</u> <u>three</u>.

3, 6, 9, __12__, __15__, __18__

1.   1, 2, 3, _____, _____, _____

2.   2, 4, 6, 8, _____, _____, _____

3.   10, 20, 30, _____, _____, _____

4.   5, 10, 15, 20, _____, _____, _____

5.   3, 6, 9, 12, _____, _____, _____

6.   20, 19, 18, 17, _____, _____, _____

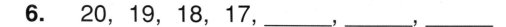

Math Connection—Grade 2—RBP3780   www.summerbridgeactivities.com   ©RBP Books

Multiplication

Draw marbles in each bag. Then solve the problem.

Multiplication is the fastest way to add equal groups. 3 x 2 is the same as 2 + 2 + 2, or 3 groups of 2.

Don't lose your marbles!

1.

4 bags. 2 marbles in each bag.

4 x 2 = _____

2.

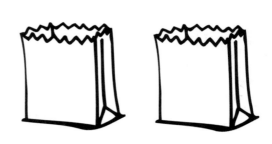

2 bags. 4 marbles in each bag.

2 x 4 = _____

3.

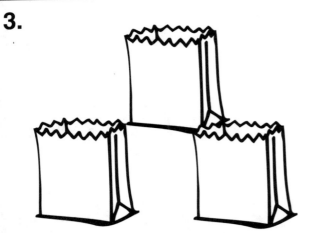

3 bags. 4 marbles in each bag.

3 x 4 = _____

4.

4 bags. 3 marbles in each bag.

4 x 3 = _____

RBP Books   www.summerbridgeactivities.com   Math Connection—Grade 2—RBP3780

Multiplication

Solve the problems.

Multiplication is the fastest way to add the same number.

Phew! That was some fast counting!

1. 3
    3   3
  + 3 x 3
   9   **9**

2. 2
    2   2
  + 2 x 3

3. 4
    4   4
  + 4 x 3

4. 5
    5   5
  + 5 x 3

5. 3
    3
    3
    3   3
  + 3 x 5

6. 2
    2
    2
    2   2
  + 2 x 5

7. 1
    1
    1
    1   1
  + 1 x 5

8. 4
    4
    4
    4   4
  + 4 x 5

9. 4
    4
    4   4
  + 4 x 4

10. 2
    2
    2   2
  + 2 x 4

11. 3
    3
    3   3
  + 3 x 4

12. 1
    1
    1   1
  + 1 x 4

Math Connection—Grade 2—RBP3780   www.summerbridgeactivities.com   ©RBP Books

Multiplication

Solve the problems.

 Look for patterns.   ?

1. 3 x 0 = __**0**__
3 x 1 = _____
3 x 2 = _____
3 x 3 = _____
3 x 4 = _____
3 x 5 = _____
3 x 6 = _____
3 x 7 = _____
3 x 8 = _____
3 x 9 = _____

2. 5 x 0 = _____
5 x 1 = _____
5 x 2 = _____
5 x 3 = _____
5 x 4 = _____
5 x 5 = _____
5 x 6 = _____
5 x 7 = _____
5 x 8 = _____
5 x 9 = _____

3. 0 x 0 = _____
0 x 1 = _____
0 x 2 = _____
0 x 3 = _____
0 x 4 = _____
0 x 5 = _____
0 x 6 = _____
0 x 7 = _____
0 x 8 = _____
0 x 9 = _____

4. 1 x 0 = _____
1 x 1 = _____
1 x 2 = _____
1 x 3 = _____
1 x 4 = _____
1 x 5 = _____
1 x 6 = _____
1 x 7 = _____
1 x 8 = _____
1 x 9 = _____

5. 4 x 0 = _____
4 x 1 = _____
4 x 2 = _____
4 x 3 = _____
4 x 4 = _____
4 x 5 = _____
4 x 6 = _____
4 x 7 = _____
4 x 8 = _____
4 x 9 = _____

6. 2 x 0 = _____
2 x 1 = _____
2 x 2 = _____
2 x 3 = _____
2 x 4 = _____
2 x 5 = _____
2 x 6 = _____
2 x 7 = _____
2 x 8 = _____
2 x 9 = _____

Multiplication

Solve the problems.

 It helps to picture multiplication in groups.
4 x 2 is four groups of two. I can see in my
mind that four groups of two is eight.

○ ○ ○ ○
○ ○ ○ ○

1.
```
   3        2        4        1        2        3
  x 3      x 1      x 4      x 5      x 3      x 4
```

2.
```
   1        3        1        5        4        3
  x 4      x 2      x 1      x 5      x 3      x 5
```

3.
```
   2        4        1        3        5        4
  x 5      x 2      x 3      x 7      x 2      x 1
```

4.
```
   2        5        3        2        7        5
  x 9      x 8      x 8      x 7      x 5      x 8
```

5.
```
   5        4        5        4        3        4
  x 6      x 8      x 9      x 6      x 9      x 7
```

Math Connection—Grade 2—RBP3780   www.summerbridgeactivities.com   © RBP Books

Multiplication

Solve the problems.

 Memorize these facts. Circle the ones you already know.

Hey, the 10s and 11s are easy!

1. 6 x 0 = _____	**2.** 7 x 0 = _____	**3.** 8 x 0 = _____
6 x 1 = _____	7 x 1 = _____	8 x 1 = _____
6 x 2 = _____	7 x 2 = _____	8 x 2 = _____
6 x 3 = _____	7 x 3 = _____	8 x 3 = _____
6 x 4 = _____	7 x 4 = _____	8 x 4 = _____
6 x 5 = _____	7 x 5 = _____	8 x 5 = _____
6 x 6 = _____	7 x 6 = _____	8 x 6 = _____
6 x 7 = _____	7 x 7 = _____	8 x 7 = _____
6 x 8 = _____	7 x 8 = _____	8 x 8 = _____
6 x 9 = _____	7 x 9 = _____	8 x 9 = _____
4. 9 x 0 = _____	**5.** 10 x 0 = _____	**6.** 11 x 0 = _____
9 x 1 = _____	10 x 1 = _____	11 x 1 = _____
9 x 2 = _____	10 x 2 = _____	11 x 2 = _____
9 x 3 = _____	10 x 3 = _____	11 x 3 = _____
9 x 4 = _____	10 x 4 = _____	11 x 4 = _____
9 x 5 = _____	10 x 5 = _____	11 x 5 = _____
9 x 6 = _____	10 x 6 = _____	11 x 6 = _____
9 x 7 = _____	10 x 7 = _____	11 x 7 = _____
9 x 8 = _____	10 x 8 = _____	11 x 8 = _____
9 x 9 = _____	10 x 9 = _____	11 x 9 = _____

RBP Books   www.summerbridgeactivities.com   Math Connection—Grade 2—RBP3780

Multiplication

Solve the problems.

1.

1	2	3	4	5	6
$\times 1$	$\times 2$	$\times 3$	$\times 4$	$\times 5$	$\times 6$

2.

7	8	9	3	4	5
$\times 7$	$\times 8$	$\times 9$	$\times 4$	$\times 5$	$\times 6$

3.

6	7	8	6	7	8
$\times 7$	$\times 8$	$\times 9$	$\times 4$	$\times 5$	$\times 6$

4.

9	3	7	6	9	4
$\times 7$	$\times 6$	$\times 6$	$\times 5$	$\times 8$	$\times 8$

5.

6	7	8	6	9	8
$\times 8$	$\times 9$	$\times 7$	$\times 3$	$\times 3$	$\times 3$

Math Connection—Grade 2—RBP3780   www.summerbridgeactivities.com   ©RBP Books

Answer Pages

Diagnostic Test 1—Page 4
1. 8   9   7   10   10   5
2. 1   5   3   6   2   3
3. 12   14   16   18   20   13
4. 5   8   6   8   7   9
5. 2 tens, 4 ones   **6.** 7 tens, 2 ones
7. 35
8. 76
9. 2   4   6   8   10
10. 22   44   56   68   70   86

Diagnostic Test 2—Page 5
1. 54¢   **2.** 62¢   **3.** 63¢   **4.** 91¢
5. 17   17   18   18   17   15
6. 11   7   7   6   9   9
7. 12   14   15   13   13   17
8. 2:20   **9.** 4:45   **10.** 10:35

Diagnostic Test 3—Page 6
1. 36   57   57   88   69   66
2. 64   63   34   25   22   26
3. 71   83   81   64   73   46
4. 39   57   19   38   55   51
5. $3.82   **6.** $2.54

Diagnostic Test 4—Page 7
1. 2 hundreds, 4 tens, 9 ones
2. 8 hundreds, 0 tens, 3 ones
3. 479
4. 900
5. <   **6.** >   **7.** <   **8.** >
9. 944   978   377   787   494
10. 520   242   752   512   132

Diagnostic Test 5—Page 8
1. 366   902   819   613   980
2. 614   714   119   307   423
3. 8   6   15   20   3   8
4. 2 inches   **5.** 3 inches
6. $\frac{1}{2}$ **7.** $\frac{3}{4}$
8. $\frac{1}{4}$ **9.** circle
10. triangle

Page 10
1. 8 tens 3 ones is the same as 83
2. 3 tens 7 ones is the same as 37
3. 4 tens 1 one is the same as 41
4. 2 tens 6 ones is the same as 26
5. 7 tens 8 ones is the same as 78
6. 1 ten 3 ones is the same as 13
7. 9 tens 2 ones is the same as 92
8. 3 tens 3 ones is the same as 33
9. 6 tens 5 ones is the same as 65

Page 11
1. 4 tens 4 ones = 44   **2.** 3 tens 7 ones = 37
3. 2 tens 8 ones = 28   **4.** 6 tens 2 ones = 62
5. 8 tens 4 ones = 84   **6.** 7 tens 3 ones = 73

Page 12

0	1	2	3	4	5	6	7	8	9
10	11	12	13	14	15	16	17	18	19
20	21	22	23	24	25	26	27	28	29
30	31	32	33	34	35	36	37	38	39
40	41	42	43	44	45	46	47	48	49
50	51	52	53	54	55	56	57	58	59
60	61	62	63	64	65	66	67	68	69
70	71	72	73	74	75	76	77	78	79
80	81	82	83	84	85	86	87	88	89
90	91	92	93	94	95	96	97	98	99

Page 13
1. 1   10   6   4   9   12
2. 5   0   11   7   2   8
3. 3   14   30   16   50   20
4. 31   13   43   89   24   92
5. 75   29   67   18   68   52
6. 99   15   88   100   17   54

Page 14
1. 19   17   12   18
2. 10   11   31   15
3. 79   94   26   87
4. 20   25   40
5. 21   84   39
6. 86   67   39

Page 15
1. Denise   **2.** Matt   **3.** Rob   **4.** Allie   **5.** Tanner

Page 16
1. 3 hundreds 3 tens 2 ones = 332
2. 2 hundreds 1 ten 6 ones = 216
3. 1 hundred 4 tens 3 ones = 143
4. 6 hundreds 3 tens 6 ones = 636
5. 4 hundreds 0 tens 5 ones = 405
6. 9 hundreds 3 tens 0 ones = 930

Page 17
1. 1 hundred 2 tens 9 ones
2. 9 hundreds 3 tens 6 ones
3. 4 hundreds 6 tens 2 ones
4. 2 hundreds 4 tens 8 ones
5. 3 hundreds 2 tens 0 ones
6. 8 hundreds 6 tens 3 ones
7. 264   **8.** 782   **9.** 914
10. 153   **11.** 305   **12.** 376

Page 18
1. 834 square around 3, circle around 4
2. 527 triangle around 5, circle around 2
3. 909 square around first 9, circle around second 9
4. 241 circle around 2, square around 4, triangle around 1
5. 156 circle around 5, triangle around 6
6. 317 square around 3, 1 crossed out, circle around 7
7. 662 square around first 6, second 6 crossed out, triangle around 2
8. 485 circle around 4, square around 5

Page 19
1. 346   214   680   **2.**   527   428   722
3. 831   400   399   **4.**   730   479   600
5. 292   872   735   **6.**   798   588   501
7. 122   701   400   **8.**   422   130   791
9. 986   700   440   **10.**   843   990   288

Page 20
1. 434   **2.** 765   **3.** 832   **4.** 790
5. 210   **6.** 874   **7.** 621   **8.** 909
9. 119   **10.** 345   **11.** 810   **12.** 923
13. 608   **14.** 599   **15.** 218   **16.** 710

Page 21
1. <   **2.** <   **3.** >   **4.** >
5. <   **6.** =   **7.** <   **8.** <
9. <   **10.** =

Page 22
1. 4 tens 6 ones, 46
2. 7 tens 3 ones, 73
3. 2 hundreds 5 tens 5 ones, 255
4. 3 tens 7 ones
5. 8 tens 0 ones
6. 5 hundreds 1 ten 3 ones
7. 9 hundreds 0 tens 2 ones
8. 2   **9.** 4   **10.** nine   **11.** six
12. 43   **13.** 48   **14.** 920   **15.** 570
16. 17, 18, 19, 20, 21
17. 254, 255, 256, 257, 258
18. 332, 333, 334, 335, 336

Page 23
1. 3 tens 2 ones, 32
2. 8 tens 4 ones, 84
3. 1 hundred 2 tens 3 ones, 123
4. 2 tens 8 ones
5. 6 tens 4 ones
6. 4 hundreds 0 tens 8 ones
7. 7 hundreds 6 tens 2 ones
8. 3   **9.** 8   **10.** ten   **11.** twenty-four
12. 59   **13.** 72   **14.** 555   **15.** 212
16. 15, 16, 17, 18, 19
17. 176, 177, 178, 179, 180
18. 259, 260, 261, 262, 263

Page 24

+	0	1	2	3	4	5	6	7	8	9	10
0	0	1	2	3	4	5	6	7	8	9	10
1	1	2	3	4	5	6	7	8	9	10	11
2	2	3	4	5	6	7	8	9	10	11	12
3	3	4	5	6	7	8	9	10	11	12	13
4	4	5	6	7	8	9	10	11	12	13	14
5	5	6	7	8	9	10	11	12	13	14	15
6	6	7	8	9	10	11	12	13	14	15	16
7	7	8	9	10	11	12	13	14	15	16	17
8	8	9	10	11	12	13	14	15	16	17	18
9	9	10	11	12	13	14	15	16	17	18	19
10	10	11	12	13	14	15	16	17	18	19	20

Page 25
1. the number
    3   6   8   9   4
2. one more than the number
    5   8   6   3   2
3. one ten and the number
    12   16   18   19   15
4. one less than ten and the number
    11   15   17   18   14

Page 26
1. 0   2   4   6   8   10
   12   14   16   18   20
2. skip counting by 2s
3. 18   14   12   4   8
4. 16   2   6   20   10

Page 27
1. 5   4   10   8   7
2. 6   10   5   8   5
3. 7   10   3   9   6
4. 5   9   4   10   10
5. 6   3   6   8   5
6. 2   9   10   9   10

Page 28
1. 3 + 5 = 8   **2.** 6 + 4 = 10
3. 6 + 3 = 9   **4.** 7 + 2 = 9

Page 29
1. 14   15   16   14   13
2. 18   17   16   13   13
3. 17   15   16   14   15
4. 11   16   14   13   11
5. 18   17   13   15   16
6. 18   15   11   16   14

Page 30
1. 7 + 6 = 13 Nick ate 13 nuts.
2. 3 + 8 = 11 Rachel had 13 pieces of bubble gum.
3. 4 + 9 = 13 Josh has 13 train cars.
4. 5 + 9 = 14 Nate played for 14 minutes.
5. 7 + 8 = 15 Mrs. White has 15 cats.
6. 9 + 8 = 17 Jeff has 17 pieces of fruit left to sell.

Page 31
1. 2 + 5 = 7   5 + 2 = 7   7 − 5 = 2   7 − 2 = 5
2. 8 + 2 = 10   2 + 8 = 10   10 − 2 = 8   10 − 8 = 2
3. 4 + 2 = 6   2 + 4 = 6   6 − 2 = 4   6 − 4 = 2
4. 3 + 8 = 11   8 + 3 = 11   11 − 3 = 8   11 − 8 = 3
5. 8 + 5 = 13   5 + 8 = 13   13 − 8 = 5   13 − 5 = 8
6. 3 + 7 = 10   7 + 3 = 10   10 − 7 = 3   10 − 3 = 7
7. 7 + 4 = 11   4 + 7 = 11   11 − 4 = 7   11 − 7 = 4
8. 6 + 3 = 9   3 + 6 = 9   9 − 6 = 3   9 − 3 = 6

Page 32
1. 4 + 5 = 9   **2.** 7 + 3 = 10   **3.** 7 + 6 = 13
   5 + 4 = 9   3 + 7 = 10   6 + 7 = 13
   9 − 4 = 5   10 − 3 = 7   13 − 6 = 7
   9 − 5 = 4   10 − 7 = 3   13 − 7 = 6
4. 7 + 8 = 15   **5.** 2 + 6 = 8   **6.** 8 + 9 = 17
   8 + 7 = 15   6 + 2 = 8   9 + 8 = 17
   15 − 8 = 7   8 − 2 = 6   17 − 9 = 8
   15 − 7 = 8   8 − 6 = 2   17 − 8 = 9
7. 6 + 8 = 14   **8.** 7 + 5 = 12
   8 + 6 = 14   5 + 7 = 12
   14 − 8 = 6   12 − 5 = 7
   14 − 6 = 8   12 − 7 = 5

Page 33
1. 9   0   6   3   6
2. 1   1   3   6   4
3. 2   5   3   6   4
4. 4   1   1   0   2
5. 8   5   3   0   8
6. 0   1   7   2   0

Page 34
1. 9 − 2 = 7 children   **2.** 8 − 2 = 6 cars
3. 6 − 3 = 3 books   **4.** 7 − 4 = 3 years old

Page 35
1. 7   6   12   0   11
2. 6   14   7   4   13
3. 5   6   11   7   7
4. 9   11   5   9   3
5. 17   5   13   9   4
6. 2   7   11   6   3

Page 36
1. 13 − 9 = 4 – Dan kept 4 puppies.
2. 18 − 9 = 9 – Max has 9 marbles left.
3. 12 − 7 = 5 – Jane can still wear 5 dresses.
4. 17 − 8 = 9 – Jim has 9 cows left.
5. 13 − 6 = 7 – Mother has 7 pieces of mail still to open.
6. 11 − 8 = 3 – Gina has lost 3 hair ribbons.

(124)

Answer Pages

Page 37
1.	3	3	10	1	2
2.	5	4	8	1	1
3.	10	3	0	5	1
4.	3	7	2	0	5
5.	9	4	3	6	10
6.	2	10	10	0	2

Page 38
1. 5 − 3 = 2 pink roses   2.   8 + 3 = 11cats in all
3. 2 + 7 = 9 things   4.   10 − 7 = 3 nuts left
5. 10 − 6 = 4 crayons are not broken
6. 6 + 3 = 9 carrots in all

Page 39
1.	9	10	12	15	16	13
2.	13	14	9	14	9	18
3.	8	12	15	13	5	5
4.	14	8	16	7	9	18
5.	18	3	17	8	15	6
6.	14	18	11	9	16	18

Page 40
1.	10	15	13	13	14	11
2.	11	14	17	12	9	11
3.	13	12	10	13	13	16
4.	8	3	8	6	6	9
5.	8	7	7	7	5	3
6.	8	8	5	4	6	6

Page 41
1. 6 + 8 = 14 Pat has 14 pets.
2. 11 − 7 = 4 The dog has 4 bones left.
3. 6 + 8 = 14 Josie ran for 14 minutes.
4. 15 − 6 = 9 Brock has 9 jars left.
5. 12 − 5 = 7 Chan has 7 cookies left.
6. 4 + 9 = 13 Mary picked 13 apples.

Page 42
1.	15	10	12	9	11	12
2.	11	10	14	8	12	12
3.	18	13	13	11	16	11
4.	7	6	9	7	5	4
5.	9	8	8	9	8	4
6.	5	6	4	8	10	6

Page 43
1.	13	11	11	11	18	11
2.	10	12	15	12	14	17
3.	15	12	15	14	17	9
4.	3	5	5	8	4	3
5.	6	7	10	8	6	6
6.	7	4	6	8	7	4

Page 44
1.   22¢   2.   45¢   3.   80¢

Page 45
1.   50¢   2.   35¢   3.   40¢
4.   55¢   5.   52¢   6.   80¢

Page 46
1.   65¢   2.   70¢   3.   60¢
4.   81¢   5.   75¢   6.   90¢

Page 47
A.   72¢ – truck   B.   90¢ – ring
C.   77¢ – ball   D.   41¢ – balloon
E.   63¢ – necklace   F.   58¢ – drums

Page 48
1. 1 half-dollar, 2 dimes, 3 pennies
2. 1 half-dollar, 1 quarter, 1 nickel, 4 pennies
3. 1 half-dollar, 1 quarter, 1 dime, 1 nickel, 1 penny
4. 1 half-dollar, 1 penny
5. 1 quarter, 1 dime, 4 pennies
6. 2 dimes, 2 pennies
7. 1 quarter, 1 dime, 1 nickel, 3 pennies
8. 1half-dollar, 1 dime, 1 nickel, 4 pennies
9. 1 quarter, 2 dimes
10. 1 half-dollar, 1 dime, 2 pennies

Page 49
1. $1.50   2. $1.70   3. $1.42
4. $2.64   5. $2.86   6. $3.60

Page 50
1. circle 1 dollar and 1 quarter
2. circle 1 dollar, 1 quarter, 2 dimes, and 2 pennies
3. circle 3 quarters, 1 nickel, and 2 pennies
4. circle 1 dollar, 4 quarters, 3 dimes, 1 nickel

Page 51
1.   60¢ no   2.   50¢ yes   3.   95¢ yes
4.   29¢ no   5.   80¢ no   6.   49¢ no

Page 52
1.   9:00   2.   minute   3.   the hour hand
4.   5   5.   60   6.   12
7.   30   8.   24

Page 53
1.   3:00   2.   2:30   3.   7:30
4.   12:30   5.   11:00   6.   6:00

Page 54
1.   2.   3.
4.   5.   6.

Page 55
1.   2:15   2.   1:35   3.   12:05
4.   8:10   5.   6:25   6.   3:10

Page 56
1.   2.   3.
4.   5.   6.

Page 57
1.   12:00   2.   9:15   3.   2:10
4.   3:45   5.   30 minutes   6.   4:15

Page 58
1.   48¢   2.   77¢   3. $2.56   4. $1.62
5.   4:15   6.   6:45   7.   3:20   8. 10:55

Page 59
1.   67¢   2.   83¢   3. $2.64   4. $1.92
5.   3:30   6.   5:15   7.   4:25   8. 10:10

Page 60
1. 14 7 18 12 12
2. 12 18 16 16 17
3. 8 12 9 18 18
4. 18 18 19 20 15

Page 61
1. 4 + 6 + 9 = 19 worms
2. 13 + 11 + 20 = 44 ears of corn
3. 7 + 6 + 4 = 17 dogs
4. 6 + 11 + 12 = 29 people left
5. 23 + 14 + 31 = 68 buttons
6. 14 + 11 + 21 = 46 pencils

Page 62
1. 35 28 53 39 39
2. 29 56 96 75 85
3. 69 66 97 19 39
4. 28 39 84 35 92
5. 35 44 35 18 47
6. 20 96 99 49 99

Page 63
1. 25 39 56 89 77
2. 58 57 98 89 59
3. 57 68 46 68 97
4. 77 89 68 87 44
5. 58 79 99 49 78
6. 94 74 85 38 72

Page 64
1. 10 40 51 31 55
2. 14 20 23 13 10
3. 6 16 50 23 44
4. 3 51 13 40 22
5. 1 10 52 51 16
6. 12 20 2 5 31

Page 65
1. 46 13 21 43 31
2. 34 53 61 42 53
3. 43 31 21 55 21
4. 23 26 15 53 20
5. 28 31 25 61 35
6. 31 43 21 24 31

Page 66
1. 64 57 96 29 42
2. 40 97 90 54 22
3. 19 13 99 31 69
4. 21 20 10 39 11
5. 23 34 16 99 21
6. 2 99 44 40 27

Page 67
1. 38 75 97 79 89
2. 96 79 59 85 88
3. 99 85 84 87 59
4. 12 66 31 61 42
5. 46 22 32 42 26
6. 21 16 52 23 32

Page 68
1. 35 + 33 = 68 children
2. 75 − 63 = 12 seats left
3. 37 − 23 = 14 acorns left
4. 24 + 32 = 56 pieces
5. 53 − 41 = 12 more cards
6. 48 − 6 = 42 cookies left

Page 69
1. 48 75 85 49 66
2. 76 95 99 82 54
3. 69 75 87 57 69
4. 44 24 50 31 65
5. 34 31 54 64 12
6. 34 13 22 25 32

Page 70
1. 87 77 88 48 86
2. 67 78 78 77 67
3. 79 88 73 57 66
4. 25 34 63 81 63
5. 22 38 41 40 72
6. 52 15 27 32 41

Page 71
1. 1 ten 2 ones
2. 1 ten 6 ones
3. 1 ten 4 ones
4. 1 ten 0 ones
5. 61 112 71 91
6. 83 83 81 83

Page 72
1. 86 70 81 63 36
2. 62 41 60 92 33
3. 96 94 93 33 85
4. 40 84 74 48 81
5. 81 64 23 120 81

Page 73
1. 35 30 133 62 92
2. 42 92 86 50 57
3. 50 151 22 95 136
4. 93 37 106 121 100
5. 111 143 134 121 104

Page 74
1. 26 61 156 42 133
2. 122 85 29 57 124
3. 68 120 68 37 80
4. 73 37 78 91 50
5. 96 114 58 55 98
6. 83 130 94 72 67

Page 75
Down
1. 115   **2.** 126   **3.** 120   **4.** 12
7. 13   **8.** 284   **12.** 531   **13.** 86
14. 13
Across
1. 117   **2.** 16   **4.** 106   **5.** 100
6. 70   **7.** 1,047   **9.** 13   **10.** 57
11. 45   **12.** 598   **13.** 86   **15.** 100

Page 76
1. 88 + 19 = 107 flowers
2. 39 + 49 = 88¢
3. 24 + 69 = 93 peanuts
4. 49 + 35 = 84¢
5. 19 + 14 = 33 worms
6. 47 + 15 = 62 tapes

Page 77
1. 19 19 17 29 57
2. 59 46 38 12 17
3. 29 9 8 19 15
4. 28 17 37 39 18

126

Answer Pages

Page 78
1.	68	45	29	17	14
2.	48	15	56	28	14
3.	26	39	46	64	62
4.	28	37	59	58	13
5.	18	26	36	35	42

Page 79
1.	12	11	14	45	33
2.	28	25	50	39	27
3.	18	8	10	28	69
4.	38	19	47	12	33
5.	68	40	28	18	47

Page 80
1.	12	12	3	12	11
2.	28	17	17	58	17
3.	26	26	18	26	26
4.	25	29	28	39	78
5.	52	29	52	54	65

Page 81
1.	63	19	19	19	19
2.	35	13	32	17	13
3.	42	48	16	14	42
4.	19	29	33	27	18
5.	76	25	25	35	25
6.	59	28	59	41	57

Page 82
1. 84 − 68 = 16 peaches
2. 78 − 29 = 49 more bottle caps
3. 86 − 19 = 67 children in the pool
4. 42 − 14 = 28 cans on the shelf
5. 67 − 41 = 26 more crackers
6. 52 − 14 = 38 dominoes

Page 83
1.	81	95	100	93	62
2.	114	90	102	115	97
3.	110	113	81	112	110
4.	65	45	21	46	48
5.	38	34	53	59	43
6.	38	27	18	16	39

Page 84
1.	93	83	121	127	84
2.	87	103	92	131	88
3.	105	134	65	122	121
4.	52	59	34	37	26
5.	33	26	56	29	48
6.	42	47	18	46	19

Page 85
1. 36 + 45 = 81 problems completed
2. 36 − 7 = 29 problems correct
3. 81 + 37 = 118 problems completed
4. 27 − 19 = 8 students
5. 96 − 39 = 57 papers left
6. 25 + 34 + 27 = 86 problems so far

Page 86
1.	95	96	75	101	62
2.	102	100	87	88	95
3.	121	120	81	112	110
4.	46	35	21	45	40
5.	28	24	27	49	31
6.	17	36	32	48	39

Page 87
1.	77	94	73	104	70
2.	121	114	75	107	98
3.	95	113	102	121	124
4.	47	26	43	57	18
5.	39	45	49	28	16
6.	36	28	48	47	29

Page 88
1.	11	**2.**	Luis	**3.**	Juan
4.	Pedro	**5.**	31 books		

Page 89
1.	July	**2.**	Thursday	**3.**	Sunday
4.	31	**5.**	5	**6.**	17 days

Page 90
1.	9	**2.**	11	**3.**	6	**4.**	9

Page 91
1. first − circle   **2.** third − square
3. second − circle   **4.** third − rectangle

Page 92
1. first − tablespoon   **2.** second − gallon
3. third − 2 quart carton   **4.** first − 1 cup

Page 93
1. 6 inches   **2.** 2 inches
3. 3 inches   **4.** 5 inches

Page 94
1. 2 + 2 + 2 + 2 = 8
2. 1 + 1 + 1 + 1 + 1 + 1 = 6
3. 3 + 2 + 3 + 2 = 10
4. 3 + 3 + 2 = 8

Page 95
1. 10 cm   **2.** 13 cm
3. 11 cm   **4.** 4 cm
5. 7 cm
6. 4 + 2 + 4 + 2 = 12 cm
7. 5 + 5 + 8 = 18 cm
8. 5 + 1 + 5 + 1 = 12 cm

Page 96
Answers will vary.

Page 97
1.	726	963	976	825	927
2.	500	677	153	575	368
3.	973	999	697	666	358
4.	969	178	758	863	900
5.	797	788	797	776	252

Page 98
1.	328	764	475	179	781
2.	326	403	963	599	277
3.	798	758	271	327	939
4.	362	785	837	896	507
5.	360	882	413	569	642

Page 99
1. 346 + 416 = 762 students
2. 236 + 127 = 363 students
3. 119 + 57 = 176 students
4. 318 + 229 = 547 students
5. 112 + 124 = 236 kindergartners
6. 212 + 178 = 390 books

Answer Pages

Page 100
1.	741	153	507	584	624
2.	375	130	238	710	50
3.	114	521	321	114	550
4.	450	212	521	242	630
5.	121	343	111	301	747

Page 101
1.	394	308	398	209	575
2.	278	802	625	491	408
3.	469	84	516	396	149
4.	688	738	305	148	478
5.	106	146	167	113	186

Page 102
1. 427 − 109 = 318 cards left
2. 264 − 175 = 89 more cards
3. 822 − 800 = 22 pennies left
4. 947 − 731 = 216 more caps
5. 540 − 421 = 119 less dollars
6. 127 − 82 = 45 dollars

Page 103
1.	434	193	599	939	11
2.	378	286	966	99	917
3.	381	49	588	841	201
4.	789	206	255	499	270
5.	198	559	234	211	472

Page 104
1.	709	557	919	797	1,032
2.	563	349	333	238	439
3.	459	951	711	624	1,157
4.	547	354	286	621	339
5.	1,570	375	165	690	986

Page 105
1.	682	680	575	719	1,086
2.	517	513	445	549	378
3.	682	649	1,044	915	1,020
4.	304	89	293	567	172
5.	503	585	994	587	569

Page 106
1. 324 + 271 = 595 **2.** 452 − 241 = 211
3. 332 + 164 = 496 **4.** 567 + 325 = 242
5. 724 − 510 = 214

Page 107
1.	566	884	467	498	599
2.	721	929	922	1,024	1,325
3.	763	675	611	343	454
4.	414	665	588	537	292

5. 334 + 249 = 583 miles
6. 802 − 789 = 13 pennies

Page 108
1.	566	663	447	668	397
2.	923	825	1,082	841	1,071
3.	671	615	372	246	742
4.	328	546	540	538	118

5. 368 − 299 = 69 cards
6. 298 + 479 = 777 cans

Page 109
1. $\frac{1}{4}$ 2. $\frac{1}{2}$ 3. $\frac{3}{4}$ 4. $\frac{3}{4}$ 5. $\frac{2}{3}$ 6. $\frac{1}{3}$

Page 110
1. $\frac{1}{4}$ 2. $\frac{1}{2}$ 3. $\frac{2}{4}$ 4. $\frac{3}{4}$ 5. $\frac{2}{3}$ 6. $\frac{1}{3}$

Page 111
1. $\frac{1}{2}$ 2. $\frac{3}{4}$ 3. $\frac{5}{8}$ 4. $\frac{1}{4}$

Page 112

1. 2. 3. 4. 5. 6.

Page 113
1. red **2.** blue **3.** orange and yellow **4.** green

Page 114
Answers will vary.

Page 115
1.	circle	**2.**	square	**3.**	circle
4.	square	**5.**	star	**6.**	star

Page 116
1.	4, 5, 6	**2.**	10, 12, 14	**3.**	40, 50, 60
4.	25, 30, 35	**5.**	15, 18, 21	**6.**	16, 15, 14

Page 117
1. 8 **2.** 8 **3.** 12 **4.** 12

Page 118
1. 9, 9	**2.** 6, 6	**3.** 12, 12	**4.** 15, 15
5. 15, 15	**6.** 10, 10	**7.** 5, 5	**8.** 20, 20
9. 16, 16	**10.** 8, 8	**11.** 12, 12	**12.** 4, 4

Page 119
1.	0	3	6	9	12
	15	18	21	24	27
2.	0	5	10	15	20
	25	30	35	40	45
3.	0	0	0	0	0
	0	0	0	0	0
4.	0	1	2	3	4
	5	6	7	8	9
5.	0	4	8	12	16
	20	24	28	32	36
6.	0	2	4	6	8
	10	12	14	16	18

Page 120
1.	9	2	16	5	6	12
2.	4	6	1	25	12	15
3.	10	8	3	21	10	4
4.	18	40	24	14	35	40
5.	30	32	45	24	27	28

Page 121
1.	0	6	12	18	24
	30	36	42	48	54
2.	0	7	14	21	28
	35	42	49	56	63
3.	0	8	16	24	32
	40	48	56	64	72
4.	0	9	18	27	36
	45	54	63	72	81
5.	0	10	20	30	40
	50	60	70	80	90
6.	0	11	22	33	44
	55	66	77	88	99

Page 122
1.	1	4	9	16	25	36
2.	49	64	81	12	20	30
3.	42	56	72	24	35	48
4.	63	18	42	30	72	32
5.	48	63	56	18	27	24